W9-AUI-892

Achieving a Safe and Reliable Product

Also available from ASQ Quality Press:

Product Safety Excellence: The Seven Elements Essential for Product Liability Prevention
Timothy A. Pine

Development of FDA-Regulated Medical Products: A Translational Approach, Second Edition
Elaine Whitmore

HALT, HASS, and HASA Explained: Accelerated Reliability Techniques, Revised Edition
Harry W. McLean

Medical Device Design and Regulation
Carl T. DeMarco

The FDA and Worldwide Quality System Requirements Guidebook for Medical Devices, Second Edition
Amiram Daniel and Ed Kimmelman

Quality Risk Management in the FDA-Regulated Industry
José Rodríguez-Pérez

The Power of Deduction: Failure Modes and Effects Analysis for Design
Michael A. Anleitner

Process Improvement Using Six Sigma: A DMAIC Guide
Rama Shankar

Root Cause Analysis: Simplified Tools and Techniques, Second Edition
Bjørn Andersen and Tom Fagerhaug

The Certified Manager of Quality/Organizational Excellence Handbook: Third Edition
Russell T. Westcott, editor

To request a complimentary catalog of ASQ Quality Press publications, call 800-248-1946, or visit our Web site at http://www.asq.org/quality-press.

Achieving a Safe and Reliable Product

A Guide to Liability Prevention

E.F. "Bud" Gookins

ASQ Quality Press
Milwaukee, Wisconsin

American Society for Quality, Quality Press, Milwaukee, WI 53203
© 2012 by ASQ
All rights reserved. Published 2012.
Printed in the United States of America.

18   17   16   15   14   13   12   5   4   3   2   1

Library of Congress Cataloging-in-Publication Data

Gookins, E. F.
Achieving a safe and reliable product: a guide to liability prevention/
E.F. "Bud" Gookins.
   p. cm.
ISBN 978-0-87389-841-6 (hardcover: alk. paper)
1. Products liability—United States. I. Title.
KF1296.G665 2012
346.7303'8—dc23
                                    2012013439

Publisher: William A. Tony
Acquisitions Editor: Matt T. Meinholz
Project Editor: Paul Daniel O'Mara
Production Administrator: Randall Benson

ASQ Mission: The American Society for Quality advances individual, organizational, and community excellence worldwide through learning, quality improvement, and knowledge exchange.

Attention Bookstores, Wholesalers, Schools, and Corporations: ASQ Quality Press books, video, audio, and software are available at quantity discounts with bulk purchases for business, educational, or instructional use. For information, please contact ASQ Quality Press at 800-248-1946, or write to ASQ Quality Press, P.O. Box 3005, Milwaukee, WI 53201-3005.

To place orders or to request ASQ membership information, call 800-248-1946. Visit our Web site at www.asq.org/quality-press.

∞ Printed on acid-free paper

Quality Press
600 N. Plankinton Ave.
Milwaukee, WI 53203-2914
E-mail: authors@asq.org

The Global Voice of Quality™

Dedication

This book is dedicated to my wife, Sandy.

Contents

Preface

Today most manufacturers in the United States and other industrialized countries are faced with competition not only from within the boundaries of their country but globally as well. The pressure of higher labor cost, higher material cost, increased infrastructure cost, and rigid regulatory and environmental requirements, issues most third world countries do not confront, has placed many American manufacturers in a precarious and disadvantaged position. Even companies that manufacture all or part of the product outside of the United States are responsible for the end use application of that product and can be sued for any injury to the end user. A U.S. distributor that only sells a product and does not participate in the manufacturing of that product can also be sued.

The United States leads the rest of the world in product lawsuits by more than twenty-to-one, and this trend does not seem to be reversing. In fact, the number of lawsuits is growing. Although some manufacturers have been negligent and many lawsuits are justifiable, many are frivolous.

Are these frivolous lawsuits fair?

Perhaps not, but until the United States legal system is changed American manufacturers will continue to be faced with the problems of "deep-pocket" assault by the plaintiff's attorneys and exposure to negative publicity. Even if the manufacturer wins the lawsuit they will be impacted with attorney's fees, expert witness expenses, and oftentimes a loss of sales revenue resulting from the negative perception of their product in the public eye. In the United States the legal system is constructed so that plaintiffs can hire an attorney on a contingency basis and pay nothing if the case is adjudicated against them, but companies must pay from the get-go to defend their case.

Clearly, this situation makes it a lot easier for plaintiffs to have their claims adjudged without an up-front cost to them. Basically, the plaintiff has nothing to lose and everything to gain. In other countries it is mandatory that the plaintiff pay the attorney's fee up front. Only at this time is

Great Britain making slow changes to accept that the plaintiff may contract with an attorney on a contingency basis, which is counterproductive in reducing the number of lawsuits worldwide.

Can United States manufacturers or distributors do anything to combat this discriminatory situation?

Short of changing legislation to restrict the monetary motivations of lawyers and their clients and placing ceilings on the amount one can be awarded, there is only one alternative for United States manufacturers and distributors. That is to develop a sound and documented *product safety, product reliability,* and *product liability prevention* system. This initiative would reduce the exposure of manufacturers and distributors to lawsuits and, more importantly, would reduce the potential for harm to the user of the product.

Clearly, one of the goals of an organization should be to provide users with a safe and reliable product, independent of compliance with legal or governmental regulations. This goal, from a moral and ethical position, should be the prime driver toward encouraging the organization to take the necessary steps to provide a safe and reliable product and to protect the end user from harm.

So why aren't most companies doing just that?

The answer is *cost.* Many organizations perceive that a product safety and reliability program will cost a lot of money to implement and sustain.

Most companies believe "product liability prevention" is an added expense over and above the cost of doing business in a highly competitive global marketplace. But this approach, although understandable in an attempt to keep cost under control, is not the wisest course to follow. All manufacturers around the world should address safety issues and assure end users of a safe and reliable product. This is a commitment and obligation that all manufacturers—and even distributors of products—should endorse.

In order to better understand the product safety process and to provide a systematic method of starting the product liability prevention journey, we must first understand the product life cycle and address each stage.

THE PRODUCT LIFE CYCLE

This can be done in four separate but sequential steps.

The product is introduced in the conceptual stage (inception). At this step someone, or team of individuals, should be assigned the job of developing a "concept design." A concept design is the formulation of an original idea into an abstract notion that shows the "stages and gates" of a complete process. For more detail see Concept Design Parameters in Chapter 1. After the diagram is developed, someone should review the product using the diagram to examine the stages and gates in order to assure no exposure exists to an unsafe product. Any concerns of product safety should be resolved at that time. This activity is the kick-off of the other three life cycle steps. Caveat: Don't assume that this function is a task to be conducted solely by the design engineering department staff. It is advisable to incorporate as many organizational disciplines as needed to assure the manufacture of a safe and reliable product.

The second step is the pre-production stage. This stage includes the review of manufacturing processes, materials, machine capability, and any other work environment or infrastructure issues that may impair the proper manufacturing and conformance of the product. This activity also includes the development of a pre-production product analysis or prototype and, where applicable, a review of all the characteristics of the product to assure conformance to the specifications and end-user environment. All non-compliances to internal or external specifications or standards must be corrected before release to production operations.

The third step is the production stage. This stage addresses the processing and evaluation of the product. Essentially, it requires compliance with the work done at the pre-production stage to assure that production processes are performing as expected. This is when the sales group can interface with the customer regarding the actual fit, form, or function of the product in the field. Sales feedback is essential. These findings permit adjustment to the processes or product design before the product is in full production.

The fourth step (last stage) is the post-production stage. This is the maturity phase; the product has been in the field for a period of time and has been exposed to the application and intended use environment. It is advisable to recognize that many application conditions change and the organization needs to be aware of these changes. This post-production stage provides for a review to assess whether changes have an adverse effect on the manufacturing or design parameters of the product.

All four stages of this product safety initiative should be assigned to qualified individuals or teams in the organization and should be carried out without bias. All issues and concerns should be documented. These four product liability prevention activities are critical in any manufacturing organization's construct, and should be an integral part of the processes. If just one of these four stages is omitted from the product safety initiative, failure may result, consequently causing harm to an end user and subjecting the company to a product liability lawsuit.

The integration of a "Product Safety Council" and other safety activities in the organization can be done without excessive cost to the manufacturer. To neglect this initiative can result in a cost that may be many times the cost of incorporating a sound product safety program. I believe that no person or manufacturer wants to produce a product that may cause harm to the end-user…be it foreseeable or unforeseeable use.

And I believe that it is in the best interest of the company, both morally and ethically, to marshal the resources to initiate this activity.

The following chapters will walk the reader though a series of product systems and design concepts that will enable the manufacturer and service organizations to establish a product safety and product liability prevention process that can be integrated into an existing structure.

Up to this point we have referenced manufactured products and we will continue to focus on the design and manufacture of fabricated products. However, throughout this book we will also incorporate the service industry into our discussions. In Chapter 10 we will dedicate our efforts to the service of the human element. Particular attention will be given to the hotel and restaurant industries and how to evaluate the product safety aspects of each. These examples can be carried over to all service type businesses.

As we go forward in the development of a product safety system we will establish a paradigm that will allow for selected activities to represent both manufactured product and service type products. Although many of the elements will apply only to a manufactured product, many will apply to both. Throughout this book when we refer to the product we can appropriately substitute a manufactured product with a service product.

Introduction

An organization can be sued for just about any reason. The suit can be for a manufacturer's defect, basically a production process deficiency; for a design defect, erroneous design criteria; or for a systemic defect, a defect of the standards, procedures, and instructions including "failure to warn." These defects can be found not only in the manufacturing industries, but in the service industries as well. The lawsuit can be for a lack of a proper material specification, lack of provision for a foreseeable or unforeseeable application, reasonable or unreasonable usage, or the organization's failure to consider the misuse or abuse of the product in its application.

Most organizations are aware of the potential problems associated with producing and selling a defective product or a product that can be subject to misuse or abuse by the consumer or user. But once a company is sued, what can it do to minimize the negative impact on the company and build a defensive case?

A company's success in defending against a product liability suit depends on two main questions. First, what is the legal expertise or knowledge of the plaintiff's attorney seeking damages for the client? Virtually all plaintiff product liability attorneys will have a product liability consultant on staff or available for defect research and/or application expertise. Attorneys will pay top dollar for these consultants because the rewards can be extremely high. In essence, the more convincing the data and information supplied by the consultant, the higher the reward. The second question is this. What is the nature of the damage, and who was injured? If the product defect caused harm or damage to the user of the product, and it can be proven that manufacturer neglect contributed to the user's injury, particularly injury to a child, senior citizen, or disabled person, the technical testimony can be quite convincing to a jury...and play on the jury's emotions.

Product litigation can be extremely expensive to a plaintiff who must bankroll a case (without attorney contingency) that will involve an expert witness to examine the product, attorney time to obtain depositions, attorney travel expenses, and attorney administration time. Win or lose, all of these costs must be paid by the plaintiff or, on a contingency basis, by the attorney. It is important that the plaintiff's attorney recognize the gravity of the lawsuit prior to submitting litigation to the court process and evaluate the potential reward to his or her client. It is against the law for an attorney to foster litigation by aiding in a lawsuit in return for a share in the proceeds. Although this subsidizing of the litigation process, a practice called "champerty," is unlawful, it is acceptable to negotiate an attorney's fee as a percentage of any reward and to negotiate a contingency partnership to pay for any ancillary expenses. This activity has become quite popular in the last several years.

But regardless whether an attorney takes the case on a contingency basis or fee structure, a great deal of money has been awarded over the last few decades to plaintiffs who take on the "big guys." These awards won't be modified unless some future ceiling is placed upon the amount one can be compensated.

Even though many are classified as "nuisance" cases and are difficult to win, they may be settled directly between opposition parties without going to trial; in other words, they are settled out of court. In most situations the defendant (the manufacturer or servicer) prefers not to endure negative publicity and the cost of defending against the nuisance case. If the case is not a nuisance but a litigation derived by harm or peril to the end user of the product, then the reward or settlement can be significantly high.

An organization that decides to sit back and do nothing to prevent or minimize a product liability lawsuit exposes itself to a very risky condition. Once a company is in a suit it's too late. But there are things an organization can do to prevent, or at least reduce, the risk of being sued. The first step is to develop a product safety checklist of do's and don'ts concerning product application, and the design and process criteria.

The second thing is to develop a "product safety council" that includes representatives from each design and manufacturing arm of the organization. Many companies today are employing an outside product safety advisor to participate in the product safety activity. The advisor will coach and guide the team to an effective construct of the activity. The final step is to establish a multi-function initiative comprising the four stages discussed in the Preface: conception, pre-production, production, and post-production.

These four stages constitute the essence of the product safety function, and once these activities have been put in place the council members can be chosen. The product safety council must include all disciplines within the organization that have either a direct effect or an indirect effect on product safety factors. Special attention must be given to possible exposure to reasonable and unreasonable applications, foreseeable and unforeseeable conditions, and possibly misuse or abuse of the product by the end user.

Each of the four stages will be discussed later in this book.

This book will also discuss the key elements of a sound operational process, quality assurance, and reliability system approach to product safety. It will address product liability prevention initiatives, the salient points involved in justifying a product recall, and how to navigate though the recall of a defective product that reaches the field.

In addition, this book will also discuss how to develop and maintain a product safety and reliability initiative in the service sector. It will look at hotel, restaurant, and cruise-ship managements as well as the construction industry.

Many business segments that historically have been excluded from product liability exposure are nevertheless candidates for causing potential harm to users; service organizations can be sued just as severely as the manufacturer of a product.

1

Design for Product Safety

In order to assure that the manufacturer has taken every precaution to provide a safe and reliable product to the end-user, we will begin the product safety journey from the design stage. In concert with this design engineering initiative we will also explore the methodologies of manufacturing processes and quality and reliability concepts. All three of these attributes must come together and work in harmony in order to provide for a final product that is safe and durable in the application and environment.

CONCEPTUAL STAGE

A new product begins with the inception of an idea. Someone, or a group of individuals, formulates an idea to produce a product. This is referred to as the conception stage. In the conception stage we begin the embryonic analysis of potential product performance characteristics. In other words, what do we expect from the new product? Will it have a reasonable life expectancy, will it be reasonably safe to the user, will it maintain a durable and reliable performance during its life, will it be user friendly, and will it have a low repair and low malfunction expectancy?

At this stage, often called "the fuzzy front end," we have an idea that can be sketched on a piece of paper and reviewed by a diversified "design review team" of individuals who represent the various core disciplines within the organizational structure. For example, representatives from design engineering, quality engineering, reliability engineering, manufacturing engineering, marketing, material management, and manufacturing processes can provide valuable inputs. Each one of these specific functions can potentially contribute specific product knowledge that otherwise could be missed.

The involvement of many different functions in the organization can provide for a holistic product design review and the assembly of a wide assortment of knowledge. Unfortunately many manufacturers are not able to secure representation from the various disciplines and must rely on a small team of design engineers to perform the conception design. This lack of broader knowledge need not limit the initiating of an effective design review with input from a product safety review team in the conceptual stage. Some common techniques can be applied, regardless whether you have a full-fledged product safety council as a juxtaposed team, comprising members of the design review team, or a small group of design and technical engineers with input from quality assurance and manufacturing personnel (three to five members).

The first step in conceptual design is to present the idea. This can be done in several ways. One way is to simply sit down and share your idea with others in the organization, perhaps your immediate supervisor or a colleague. Putting it down on paper is the most common form of idea development. You can produce a sketch including only minor details or a more detailed rendering using Unified Modeling Language (UML) or other computer aided methods such as conceptual design parameters and, if applicable, Finite Element Analysis (FEA).

With finite element analysis a computer model of a material or component is stressed and analyzed for specific results. FEA is used in new product design as well as existing product refinements. This method allows the manufacturer to verify a proposed design before releasing the product to the pre-production stage.

FEA can be used in cases of structural failure to assist in determining design changes needed to meet new requirements. It uses modeling techniques that allow the engineer to insert numerous algorithms that may allow the system to behave linearly or non-linearly. Non-linear review of many plastic products has an advantage over a linear system in that it allows for deformation of the materials used and may allow testing of the material all the way to fracture. This method of product design and testing is significantly less expensive than the cost of building and testing a new or modified product in the pre-production stage. As computer-aided techniques continue to mature, FEA software will become conjoined with faster and more reliable technologies to provide for a more refined method of predicting potential failure.

This analysis method provides a concept for testing structural, vibration, and fatigue failure and for heat transfer analysis. It solves the challenge of predicting failures caused by unknown stresses by indicating problematical areas in a material and allowing design engineers to review the theoretical stresses of a new product prior to the pre-production stage.

In addition to FEA other product design tools can be used. For example, today Design for Six Sigma (DFSS) is a separate and emerging methodology related to the widely used existing Six Sigma concepts. While traditional Six Sigma requires that a process be in place and functioning, DFSS is primarily driven by the "voice of the customer." It is process-generated rather than using Six Sigma process improvement objectives. It differs from Six Sigma in that it emphasizes the "design" concept rather than the "improvement" aspect. The traditional Six Sigma utilizes the DMAIC concept, an acronym for Define, Measure, Analyze, Improve, and Control. Design for Six Sigma utilizes the DMADV concept, an acronym for Define, Measure, Analyze, Design, and Verify.

The main goal of DFSS is to remove obstacles; it strives to generate a new process where none presently exist, or to replace an existing process that is judged to be ineffective and in need of improvement. It is a proactive and systemic method to build important customer requirements into all related aspects of the product development processes, a method that can be measured, verified, and improved.

The technique used for DFSS basically derives from system engineering philosophy, which emphasizes the customer's desire to transform expectations into a safe and reliable product at the most economical level of production. DFSS will use statistical and quantitative methods to establish conduits between system performance and customer inputs, which should provide a transition from a reactionary mode to a predictive and optimized progression mode. It is largely a design activity requiring specific techniques such as Use Cases and Interaction Design, TRIZ, Design for X, Design of Experiments (DOE), Quality Functional Deployment (QFD), Axiomatic Design, Taguchi Methods, Robustness Analysis, and Unified Modeling Language (UML).

Use Cases and Interaction Design is widely used in large projects with multi-complexity parameters and complex applications. Its purpose is to capture the functional requirements of software systems. Use Case can serve as a powerful tool for brainstorming and modeling user workflows between design and development. It is an assurance exercise applied when the developing engineer can't deduce from the prototypes what will happen when the workflow takes other paths than the successful one.

The use case indicates to the design engineer a potential event that was not considered in the entire workflow. Missing key design parameters and catching them downstream in the process can be costly and time-consuming; even worse would be missing them altogether until they are in the customer's possession. Interaction designers have the responsibility for the task workflow and therefore must describe their designs with sufficient detail in order to prevent problems from occurring.

Robustness Analysis is the bridge between analysis and the design of the product. During this step the design engineer will begin to think about the product architecture and incorporate technical strategies into the design. Essentially, it is a pictorial image of the "what" (analysis) and the "how" (design), often referred to as the robustness diagram. Essentially, it is one objective (analysis) talking to the other objective (design). Similar to the Unified Modeling Language (UML), Robustness Analysis provides an overview of the most important diagrams used in the visual modeling of computing programs.

Unified Modeling Language (UML) was developed for the prime purpose of providing designers with a stable and common language that can be used to construct computer applications. It allows the IT person to create a unified standard modeling notation. It provides several types of diagrams that should increase the ease of understanding an application under development. The most significant standard UML diagrams are: use case diagram, class diagram, state-chart diagram, sequence diagram, component diagram, activity diagram, and deployment diagram. UML can be a high-level software tool that guides the designer through an automated and integrated development process or it can be a simple, orderly way of using "napkin design" concepts (ideas sketched on a napkin or scraps of paper) to create UML diagrams and still achieve desired results.

Failure Modes & Effects Analysis (FMEA) is the most common tool used in the conceptual stage. In fact, many organizations use only FMEA for improving the use of reliability properties in the product development activities. When used properly FMEA is a valuable tool. Using it as a "stand alone" tool can cause a manufacturer to miss some of the key elements of a safely designed product. The concept of the FMEA application is broken down into two parts: the Design FMEA, and the Process FMEA.

The Design FMEA should be constructed at the conceptual stage and should prognosticate what might cause risk to the end user of the product. Similar to the Process FMEA, the Design FMEA is broken down into *detection, severity,* and *occurrence* categories. Each category has a value system, much like the Likert Scale, from "one" to "ten" in value. The ranking of "one" indicates failure is less likely to happen; "ten" indicates that failure will most likely occur.

For example, in the category *detection,* a ranking of one indicates that failure is not likely to happen. A ranking of ten indicates that failure is very likely to happen and that you will be less likely to detect the failure. These same criteria can be constructed for severity and occurrence. The product of the three categories yields a number called the "risk priority value." Action is required when a single number or a combination of numbers exceeds a specified number.

Many other conceptual tools can be used when needed, such as Fault Tree Analysis, Failure Modes and Criticality Analysis, Fault Hazard Analysis, and Preliminary Hazard Analysis. Some of these will be discussed later in the book, and have application in other product stages as well.

Concept Diagram Parameters

Once you have an idea and have completed some preliminary work, you may want to create a concept diagram. This diagram is essentially a more detailed analysis (process flow chart) of the steps needed to produce the item. You would want to incorporate types of material to be used in the fabrication of the item, some basic tolerance criteria, the manufacturing equipment needed, and any special tooling, gage devises, or other ancillary equipment required. In concert with these internal steps you would want to ask your sales and marketing department to solicit information from an existing customer or a potential customer. The "voice of the customer" (VOC) is a critical part of the process. One of the key elements of the VOC activity addresses the safety parameters and the possibility of misuse or abuse of the product application.

Concept diagrams can be a helpful tool for fine tuning operational processes from the sales function to order entry and all the way though to final shipment. Many of the external processes, such as procurement of materials and subcomponents and special processes such as heat treating and metal finishing, can also be evaluated for safety and reliability concerns.

Every cautionary step should be taken at this stage to assure the end user a reliable and safe product. At this stage there is usually no similar product to use as a model, just a concept of how the product might be produced, which makes it somewhat difficult to conceptualize. Every attempt should be made to obtain information from within the organization and outside the company to incorporate the latest in technologies and methodologies of materials, equipment, and manufacturing processes.

PRE-PRODUCTION STAGE

Once you have decided that the new product, or an existing modified product, has been assessed and found to be a candidate for further design development, you are ready to go to the next stage. The pre-production stage will address the most efficient methods of fabrication, the best tools to use, and the determination of any product testing and appraisal evaluations.

This stage is the most critical of the four. It is the time to assess the effects of the product in either a simulated environment or the real world. It is the time to fabricate the product in a prototype mode. This prototype will reflect the most economical way to manufacture the product. Equally important, it is the time to evaluate the safety and reliability aspects of the end-use application.

The underlying problem is that many manufacturers do not take sufficient time, or simply do not know how, to conduct a truly significant pre-production approval plan (PPAP). One of the best ways to assure that every step of the pre-production process is being conducted effectively is to develop a sign-off sheet that is the guideline for the process. This sign-off sheet must be reviewed and signed by an authorized individual who is trained in that particular step of the pre-production process.

In order to begin the pre-production stage it is important to identify key factors that are common to all manufactured items. The first thing that must be determined is the item's specifications. The first question that must be answered is how many parts of the final product are purchased outside the organization. Each component must be clearly identified as to the material to be used and the dimensions and/or specifications to be met. Along with these requirements you must assess the need for testing of purchased components and the type of inspection needed to assure components that meet requirements.

In concert with evaluating purchased items needed, it's necessary to consider internal fabrication. Internal ingredients include part specifications, machine processes, testing and appraisal criteria, and other parameters essential to producing the product. The initial prototype samples are inspected and tested to design parameters and to identifiable or potential environmental applications.

Once these parameters have been identified it is important to obtain as much knowledge as possible of the environment the product will be exposed to and to simulate these conditions by establishing a test specification that will best represent the application's performance. The conjugating of the simulation testing with real world conditions will determine whether any salient issues must be addressed before the product prototype is released to production. It is advisable to test the product to the total life of that product until its failure or wear out period, if possible.

A number of criteria should be considered in the pre-production stage, including:

- **Foreseeable harm**—To safeguard the user from harm a manufacturer must envision and anticipate what harm may come to the user of the product. If this product results in injury or peril to the user, the producer of the product must show objective evidence and document the evidence to assure that the producer has taken steps to correct the problem.

- **Foreseeability for safe design**—A manufacturer must be reasonably careful in planning, designing, and manufacturing a product to avoid potential harm or peril to the user of the product. When potential harm may be present and cannot be eliminated, the manufacturer of the product must warn the user of inherent dangers, properties, or characteristics of the product.

- **Unforeseeable harm**—A manufacturer must anticipate in the pre-production stage that environmental changes or modification to the product may cause harm to the user. If this harm results in injury or peril to the user of the product, the producer of the product must show objective evidence and document the evidence that they have taken steps to safeguard the user from injury or peril, or warned the user of inherent dangers of the unforeseeable harm.

- **Misuse**—Virtually every product is subject to being used in the wrong manner. The manufacturer must design the product to reasonably assure that product misuse will not occur, or to show evidence that the design and fabrication of the product has been reviewed and tested to avoid the misuse of that product. This can be done by establishing a product safety council to review and document all action taken to avoid the misuse of the product in its application.

- **Abuse**—Some products are more likely to be abused than others. For example, some people abuse a normal tire by driving a vehicle over sharp and rough terrain, causing the rubber to be sliced and cut and resulting in a flat. This could put the driver in peril. The manufacturer of the tire may want to design a tire especially for this type of terrain or at least warn the user of the potential danger of abusing the normal tire in this way. In order to minimize this risk the manufacturer should have immediate feedback at the post-production stage of all warranty problems and all field complaints to be officially addressed at the product safety review.

At the pre-production stage the manufacturer should have a brainstorming session as a part of the product safety review. This review should address abuse conditions, the need to design and fabricate the product to provide safeguards, the need to provide a proper warning regarding the product's suitability for a specific purpose, the need to contain specific safeguards, and the importance of incorporating these into the design and manufacturing parameters.

The first two stages must include an action to minimize or, even better, eliminate potential injury or peril to the end-user. The first action requires some type of initial product design review. This can be done as a formal process or simply during an ad-hoc meeting between or among design engineering and any other organizational discipline. It is recommended that even informal meetings dealing with the safety issues of a new or existing product be documented and located for easy access by any interested party.

PRODUCTION STAGE

After the pre-production stage has been achieved, the initial samples have been approved by authorized parties, and all pre-production plans have been constructed (such as the Control Plan, the Design FMEA, the Process FMEA, and any other analysis and evaluations), the production stage can be initiated.

The production stage is the time when the first production rolls off the process line. At this stage all manufacturing equipment should have been approved for specification and tolerance control and design compliance. Moreover, the process assurance must be developed to include process flow examination. In order for this stage to be effective, all quality system disciplines must come together in harmony. See the latest ISO 9001 Quality Management System (QMS) documents for specific quality requirements.

For example, purchased material and components must come into the facility on time and meet the quality characteristics. All external and internal appraisals must be acceptable and all data and document control must be met. All gages and equipment must be accurate. All in-process and final product testing and inspection must be in compliance. All identification and traceability elements must be working. All design parameters must be reviewed and signed-off on as acceptable to the latest revision, and then communicated to the fabrication and assembly operations.

All shipping documentation and packaging specifications must be correct and verified. All warning information, including implied and expressed, must be incorporated into the shipping container as a part of the product or ancillary to the product. All warranty analysis and return goods evaluations must be in place and effective.

After a sound quality management system has been established there must be a control mechanism in place to audit for compliance to that system, and a method of taking corrective actions for those items that are out of compliance. Qualified individuals certified by an external training organization should conduct this internal auditing function.

The quality management system audit should be conducted at least once a year (recommend quarterly or semi-annually). In addition to auditing and corrective action initiatives there should be in place a subsystem for preventive action and continual improvement of the existing system.

All manufacturing equipment and processes should be analyzed for their capabilities and reliability to the specifications and final compliance to the customer's requirements. This would include both external (suppliers) and internal (production) parts or components. These analysis functions should be conducted at least once a year, more frequently if needed, and should include Gauge Repeatability & Reproducibility (GRR) where applicable.

After the product has been produced and is sitting on the shipping dock, a sample of the lot size (quantity being ship to the customer) should be randomly selected for disassembly and evaluation (D & E) and must pass all dimensional and testing parameters including shipper documentations and warning information.

POST-PRODUCTION STAGE

The post-production stage is the last leg of the product safety journey. This is the time to test the product design in the environment in which it is exposed. The intention of the design is to have the product function in a specific way and suitable for a specific purpose. We want the product to function safely and we must provide specific safeguards to assure the safety features are being implemented.

After the product has been in the customer's hands for a specific period of time, the manufacturer should conduct a real life test and compare the results with earlier simulated testing. The manufacturer should determine whether the failure rate is reliable and should assess whether product reliability and safety features are meeting customer expectations.

The key points in determining whether a product will work as its design engineers intended are as follows:

- Failure of the product to function correctly

- Failure of the product to meet the minimum product life

- Failure causing premature activation of the product in the end-use environment

- Failure of a component or final product to operate in a safe condition

- Failure to function at the prescribed application resulting in injury or harm

Each of these five malfunctions can be assessed—with limitation—at the first three stages of product design and safety activities, but they cannot be fully evaluated until they are exposed and operating in the stipulated environmental conditions. This post-production stage will yield true results of all the factors involved in the design and making of the product.

It is, therefore, imperative to have a system in place to evaluate the durability, reliability, and configuration of the product in the actual application. This system should provide for quick and accurate feedback of all failures and should report on all customer complaints, regardless of how unimportant these complaints might seem. A reliability and warranty discipline should be developed to properly assess all failures in timely manner.

After a failure has been identified it should be evaluated to determine its legitimacy and the need for further investigation and information gathering. Once these actions have been completed, the next step is to take corrective action to resolve the failure and, if necessary, to recall suspicious products that are deemed to violate regulatory agencies and statute laws and products that have been determined by the manufacturer to cause harm to the end user.

In some cases failure will not actually harm the end user but the product will fail prematurely, within the warranty period or just afterward. Today many manufacturers offer an extended warranty that they allege will protect the customer if failure occurs. However, this positions product quality and reliability assurance a "chance cause" within the hands of the customer and not the manufacturer. Many customers today are turned off by this tactic; if they had a choice, they would purchase an item with a reasonable warranty period (five years or more) from another manufacturer. The post-production stage should be the mechanism for listening to the "voice of the customer." Data derived from customer complaints and product failures should be analyzed to improve customer satisfaction and provide a more reliable product. (For more detail see Chapter 14.)

SYNOPSIS OF LIFE CYCLE STAGES

All four life cycle stages should be documented; these documents and related data should be controlled to indicate findings of problematical situations or questionable conditions and the actions that were taken to modify, correct, or prevent failure from occurring. The manufacturer should continually review product safety and reliability activities in order to ensure that processes are performed effectively and adequately.

Designing for product safety and designing to minimize product liability lawsuits is a critical exercise that affects the reputation of a manufacturer and the perception customers have of it in the marketplace. A manufacturer that elects not to initiate a product safety program, encompassing the four stages of the product design concept, exposes itself to vulnerability in the mainstream of commerce, and could be subject to legal action and/or a product recall.

A product safety initiative need not be an independent discipline, although a company with a product that has the potential to harm the end user should make every effort to formalize a sound stand-alone system. But regardless of whether the product safety initiative is part of the existing design process or a stand-alone system, it should be defined as an integral part of the product safety review.

Some organizations will initiate the product safety team at the conceptual stage and carry that team all the way through the four stages of the product life cycle. The team assigns an identification number that follows the product development progress and documents concerns the team has along the way and with how they handle the resolve. Other companies feel that the team need not begin at the design inception stage; instead they take the information derived from a smaller group of design engineers (two or three) who allocate time in the "paper napkin" phase of product development. After that function has been completed, the team comes together with a project identification number to pool team knowledge and solicit ancillary input from outside the team.

Sometimes the product safety team's discussion and brainstorming sessions become fruitless "gab sessions" with little or no positive results. Some team members participate in a non-active manner and simply go along with other team members' ideas and suggestions...good or bad. (This is referred to as "groupthink.") To assure that safe products enter the marketplace, the team leader must recognize these situations, focus on safety issues, and avoid going off on tangents.

It's probably not possible to design a product that is totally free of potential harm to the user, but manufacturers should produce every product with as much built-in quality assurance and as many fail-safe systems as possible. The fewer defective products that are shipped, the less chance there is of injury or harm to users. A product can be designed to perform a function in many different applications and environments.

2
Regulatory and Statute Laws

E ven when a system has been established to formulate, obtain, and retain the documentation and records necessary to plan and implement an effective product safety program, a manufacturer should not assume that the product safety system is complete. It still requires a periodic evaluation as to the effectiveness of the system. Because changes occur in products, production methods, marketing, distribution, technological concepts, the law, and other factors, it's important to review the system on a regular basis.

These reviews may uncover errors and misinterpretations and may lead to better and more efficient methods of maintaining documentation and data retention. All of these elements form the foundation of a sound and effective quality initiative and are important factors in establishing a library of government and other regulatory agency documents. Moreover, it's essential to have a system in place to assure that the manufacturer is working to the latest revisions of these documents.

Most regulatory agencies were established in the late eighteen hundreds to safeguard the population against dangerous conditions associated with product or service failure that resulted in harm to the end user of that product or service. In 1887 the Interstate Commerce Act attempted to curb abuses by railroads that were taking advantage of customers and other entities. Powerful railroad tycoons were sometimes able to circumvent the Act, but it sent a message to an industry that federal control was in place and "Uncle Sam" was watching.

Since that time many regulatory and statute laws have been created to protect users of product or service from harm or a failure to operate correctly. For example, in 1938 the Congress passed the Food, Drug, and Cosmetic Act, authorizing the U.S. Food and Drug Administration.

Some of the most significant federal laws regarding product safety are:

1953 – Flammable Fabrics Act*
1956 – Refrigerator Safety Act*
1966 – Highway Safety Act
1969 – Child Protection and Toy Safety Act
1970 – Lead-based Paint Poison Prevention Act
1970 – Occupational Safety and Health Act
1972 – Consumer Product Safety Act (CPSA)
1975 – Federal Warranty Act (The Magnuson–Moss Warranty Act)

Superseded by the CPSA

We will confine our attention to the Food and Drug Administration, the Occupational Safety and Health Agency, the Consumer Product Safety Commission, and the Federal Warranty Act.

THE FOOD AND DRUG ADMINISTRATION – FDA (1938)

The Food and Drug Administration's (FDA) fundamental purpose is to protect public health against impure and unsafe foods, drugs, cosmetics, medical devices, and other potentially harmful products. The Food and Drug Administration has been accused of not acting fast enough in releasing new products to the consumer. Approval usually takes much longer than in other countries, often twice as long as in some European countries. In many cases the FDA ultimately rejects a product. However, the process of testing, reviewing, and confirming results after several testing replications in a simulated environment and in a real life environment has proven a lifesaver to the public.

The FDA monitors the quality of biological products, drugs, and foods as well as the manufacturer's process efficiencies, distribution center performances, and the quality capabilities of the processes. The FDA is also charged with working in a proactive mode rather than a reactionary mode by preventing nonconforming products from reaching the marketplace.

The FDA has the authority to seize or recall products it considers potentially harmful to the public if they are not withdrawn by the manufacturer. It can act to prosecute and initiate an injunction or citation against the manufacturer.

In general the Food and Drug Administration, which is the monitoring agency for cosmetic products as well, does a good job of protecting the public. However, the cosmetic industry has no requirements at this time regarding the "shelf life" of products, and some products can cause potential harm to the user if that product is used over a long period of time. Consumers are not being made aware of the time-use ability of these products and what damage they might cause to the user if they exceed a real-time shelf life.

As organizations mature in their product safety initiatives, and the governing agency becomes aware of the ancillary situation of product application, we will better protect the user of the products.

THE OCCUPATIONAL SAFETY AND HEALTH ADMINISTRATION – OSHA (1970)

This agency is charged with assuring that employers provide a safe work environment, safe tools, and work rules and procedures that allow employees to perform safely in the workplace. All employees should observe these rules and should be encouraged to alert management to potential hazard conditions.

The purpose of OSHA is "to assure so far as possible every working man and woman in the nation safe and healthful working conditions and to preserve our human resources." To implement this goal employers are required to furnish a place of employment free from recognized hazards that cause or are likely to cause death or serious physical harm to their employees.

Objective evidence of all activities involving occupational safety and health issues concerning employees, or in-house procedures and OSHA standards, should be documented and records retained for review and subject to federal inspection. OSHA authorities are directed to conduct employee safety training and education programs.

CONSUMER PRODUCT SAFETY COMMISSION – CPSC (1972)

The Consumer Product Safety Act was passed because of growing public concern about the hazards associated with some consumer products. The purpose of the Act is to protect the consumer against unreasonable and foreseeable risks of injury. The Act established and developed safety standards and continues to encourage and promote studies concerning product-related injuries.

The Commission has the responsibility and authority to require an organization to recall a product that has been deemed unreasonably hazardous. It can require the company to determine the best disposition of the product—scrap, rework, repair, or replace at cost to the manufacturer and/or distributor. The Commission also has the responsibility and authority to prohibit hazardous and unsafe products from entering the marketplace.

The CPSC does not have direct authority to prevent a product entering the marketplace prior to distribution. The manufacturer is responsible to assure that all conceptual and pre-production safety issues have been addressed and action taken to protect the end-user from an unsafe product. Only after the product has been released to the public will the CPSC intervene in any declared product malfunction that might cause harm to the user. Products that might cause harm to the user should be subject to a defined and specific product design and product safety process by the manufacturer of that product prior to its release. It is the moral and ethical responsibility of the manufacturer to develop a product safety system to meet this obligation.

The problem with charging manufacturers with responsibility for product safety is that many have not been trained in product safety and simply don't have a product safety team or even a design review committee. In fact, many manufacturers have not conducted a Design FMEA or even a basic Process FMEA. This lack of concern not only places the consumer in harm's way, but also exposes the manufacturer to a product liability lawsuit.

A study conducted by the author and the Quality Technology Institute, a division of Gookins Technologies, determined that almost 40% of recalls were for items used by and for infants and young children (based on 15 Sears and Walmart recalls over a six-month period). This is an alarming statistic. A recent recall was conducted for a drug product that was given to children as well as adults. Adults could take the prescribed dosage without harm, but the same dosage resulted in harm to children. The Consumer Product Safety Commission was able to intervene with the drug manufacturer to assure an effective safety recall.

There is still much work to be done by manufacturers in concert with the CPSC to protect the public against harm, but historical actions by both have clearly had a positive impact on consumer safety.

THE MAGNUSON–MOSS WARRANTY FEDERAL TRADE COMMISSION IMPROVEMENT ACT (1975)

In the past, consumers were subject to the manufacturer's limited warranty of a product. If the producer of that product elected not to live up to an implied warranty, there was little a consumer could do. In 1968 a government task force was created to study the servicing, repair, and durability of consumer products. It determined that some warrantors did not honor their warranties. In addition, they concluded that there was no enforcement to protect the consumer, many warranties were inadequately understood by consumers, and that some warranties were indeed deceptive.

The Magnuson–Moss Warranty Federal Trade Commission Improvement Act was a government response to these types of inadequacies. Prior to the Act the Uniform Commercial Code (UCC), a warranty law adopted by almost every state, applied only to that particular state. The Code provides for an implied warranty of the product from the seller to the buyer of that product. An *implied warranty* is defined as an inference by the manufacturer, dealer, or distributor that a product is suitable for a specific function or use and safe to be placed in the marketplace.

The Code also provides for the modification and disclaimer of implied warranties, and gives an express warranty with a subsequent general disclaimer of any implied warranties. An *express warranty* is a statement by a manufacturer, distributor, or dealer, either in writing or verbally, that the product will perform in a safe manner and that it is suitable for a specific purpose.

However, the Code may infer that the consumer is being protected by the express or implied warranty by the manufacturer, dealer, or distributor, but these warranties can be misleading and consumers may believe they are receiving some added protection when in fact they are not. The Code provides a holistic perspective and allows only for modifications and/or limitations of the damages and resolution by the consumer's usage of the product.

The primary intent of the Code was to help buyer and seller establish a common and amiable baseline for bargaining openly. Often this concept simply did not work; the consumer was left without a voice in the terms of the warranty process and had to accept the interpretation of the seller, which in most cases was to the seller's advantage.

The federal response to these inadequacies of state laws created the Commission and the subsequent Magnuson–Moss Warranty Act, which regulated what a warranty can say and how it can be said. This allowed buyers to best determine which product was right for them. Thus the Act essentially established a national uniform minimum disclosure standard for written warranties as well as a restricted disclaimer of implied warranties.

Although the Act only applies to written warranties on consumer products, it is a means of monitoring organizations that may attempt to circumvent the rules applying to disclosure, designation, and disclaimers. The Act requires that all warranties must be user friendly and clearly understood by the layperson.

OTHER FEDERAL LAWS REGARDING SAFETY

In this chapter we have confined our governing intervention activities to the Food, Drug and Cosmetic Act, the Occupational Safety and Health Act, the Consumer Product Safety Act, and the Magnuson–Moss Warranty Federal Trade Commission Improvement Act. Although these four regulations are the most familiar consumer safety regulations, other federal laws also directly affect the product safety design parameters.

Other salient safety regulations include the National Traffic and Motor Vehicle Safety Act (1966), the Fire Research and Safety Act (1968), and the Oil Protection Act of 1990 (a result of the Valdez oil spill). These Acts reflect a need to protect consumers from harm and to protect the environmental conditions of the nation.

The National Highway Traffic Safety Administration (NHTSA) also investigates reports of safety-related non-conformities and can mandate that car manufacturers take effective steps to correct defects. The National Traffic and Motor Vehicle Safety Act was established primarily to reduce the number of injuries and deaths from traffic accidents. Much like the CPSA, NHTSA can require car manufacturers to correct safety-related defects even if the defect has not caused an accident or injury to the consumer. The NHTSA also requires car manufacturers to notify the agency of any non-conformity that the manufacturer has found in its vehicles and the corrective action it intends to take.

One of the main objectives of NHTSA is to act from a proactive rather than a reactive position. The agency's primary goal is to pursue an accident-prevention policy of anticipation and resolve questionable conditions that may cause a vehicle accident resulting in harm to the buyer.

STATUTE LAW

Legislation bodies, including city, state, and federal entities, adopt *statutory laws*. These laws are designed to promulgate regulations by administrative agencies and are a part of the law governing all business activities. Statutory law is a primary law that can overturn or at least limit common law and case law.

Common law is a collection of unwritten principles, recognized and enforced by the courts, based on customs and usages of the public. Its foundation dates back many centuries to the Middle Ages in Europe. Today it is the driver for most court decisions and the moral and ethical parameters of our society.

Case law evolved from judicial decisions. It is not based on the statute or common principles of the law, but rather on the decision of the jury or judge on a "first time" judgment. This judgment, referred to as *stare decisis*, becomes a guide and precedent for future similar cases. Judges in future cases are not bound by stare decisis and may rule to a new verdict; this, in itself, may establish a new precedent.

For many manufacturers, dealers, and distributors of a product, the federal statutory law is the prime driver. This is particularly true of companies whose products cross state boundaries.

3
Product Hazards Analysis

The objective of any organization is to produce a product that has a distinct market, one that will show a profit when sold. This is true for any product that is fabricated and also for service items. But a product designed in an unsafe manner could cause harm to the end user and expose the producer to a product liability recall or possibly a lawsuit. This potential lawsuit or recall could result in the demise of the organization, or at least place the organization in a precarious situation in the marketplace…as well as with other stakeholders. Therefore, it is imperative that the organization establish a product hazard initiative designed to analyze potential hazards that may arise in the application of that product.

No product is completely safe if it is used erroneously, or used intentionally but in a hazardous environment. For example, recently a manufacturer of children's toys produced a small plastic toy in the shape of a dinosaur. A child put the toy dinosaur in his mouth and subsequently choked on it. The company's manufacturing department made the toy exactly to design parameters and the quality assurance department validated that design characteristics were met. Even so, the toy caused an injury to the user of the product.

Another example involved a "teething ring" designed to reduce the pain a baby might endure when its teeth start to develop. The teething ring was manufactured correctly and did, in fact, meet all the quality testing and inspection criteria. When the ring was used by the infant, the outer material started to break down and the toxic viscous contents eventually discharged, causing harm to the baby. Needless to say, the company was subject to a major recall.

There are endless situations like these two examples that could have been eliminated if proper product hazard analysis had been conducted as a part of the organizational product safety initiative. In a study conducted by Gookins Technologies, a product safety training and consulting firm, it was reported that on average more than 40% of all consumer recalls resulted from harm caused to children seven years old or younger. The same study was conducted on four subsequent random dates and confirmed the recalls' initial statistics.

Baby cribs that strangle infants, cars that speed out of control on their own, lead in children's toys, and lawn tractors that catch fire when exhaust pipes ignite dry grass are all examples of hazard conditions. These examples reflect questionable design parameters and the lack of a sound product hazard review. However, a product made to design characteristics and manufactured to meet all quality requirements, including critical parameter inspection and testing, might still be inherently dangerous and that could result in harm to the end user.

Examples of inherent product hazard include snow blowers and lawn mowers that could throw stones or other solid objects, injuring the user or a person nearby, or a turkey cooker that could explode when the turkey enters the pot, causing injury to someone standing near the cooker. Other items such as a nail gun, table saw, chain saw, or even a cutting knife or scissors could harm the user or someone else.

Many other factors potentially expose users to harmful conditions. Common reasons include improper or nonexistent preventive main-tenance programs in the field, poor production practices, and noncompliance of personnel to procedures or instructions. For example, an aircraft maintenance technician who fails to check for ice on the wings of an aircraft and fails to "de-ice" the plane could cause serious harm to many. Many reasons are as simple as a lack of proper notification about hazardous materials, toxic substances, flammable gases or liquids, or even prescription drugs. All of these examples will be discussed in more detail in Chapter 13.

Hazard characteristics vary in magnitude and severity. They can be classified as mechanical hazards, pressure hazards, toxic hazards, vibration hazards, chemical hazards, electrical hazards, explosive hazards, flammability hazards, and temperature hazards. Each one can be broken down into subsets. For example, mechanical hazards could include sharp edges, pointed tips, heavy weighted products, rotating products, reciprocating products, and wedged points. The objective of analyzing by categories is to not miss any possibility of determining an injury from that classification. Potential injuries in the mechanical hazards category could include cuts, bruises, broken bones, crushed body parts, strain, puncture, or a damaged eye.

Each product should be analyzed for hazard parameters from every possible position. A manufactured part should be reviewed from the component posture, the fabricated posture, and then in the final assembly. Components should be appraised for quality, whether produced in the factory or procured from a supplier, and should be inspected and tested to validate that the item is free of potential hazard conditions.

4

Manufacturing Process Analysis

Once an organization has determined that a new or modified product is worthy of pursuit and that, subsequently, the four design stages have been completed to include safeguards and safety parameters, it is important that these safety criteria be incorporated into the design. These safeguards are critical to assuring that the end user of the product is safe from harm, and that the product specifications have been considered and built into the design. These specifications have been developed to include reasonable tolerances and clear and precise types of materials to be used, including special processes such as metal finishing, heat treating, and e-coating.

However, the best design in the world cannot totally prevent a product from failing or causing harm to the end user. It takes a sound manufacturing process that is planned and capable of meeting the design characteristics. The manufacturing of a product is a key element of assuring a product will meet the intended application and be reasonably free of manufacturing defects.

Improper manufacturing techniques and a poorly controlled manufacturing process can actually create hazardous properties in the product. Non-conforming characteristics in production and/or assembly have been the reason for a number of accidents that could have been avoided if the organization had taken proper care in the planning stage of production processing.

Failure of the company to remove metal burrs, sharp edges, defective welds, and surface cracks are common examples. However, many other manufacturing conditions are just as salient as these physical characteristics. One of the main conditions is the human element, a significant contributor to the cause of potential failures. For example, a design engineer may specify a particular material to be used in the fabrication of the product, but a value engineer or purchasing manager who has not communicated with the designer may elect to change the material to a less expensive type in order to save money.

Another example is a manufacturing supervisor who bakes a sub-assembly for two hours rather than the specified four hours in order to save time. This decision by the supervisor may result in hydrogen embrittlement, causing failure in the customer application. Perhaps the most common reason for post-production failures within the manufacturing community is the assignment of untrained or inadequately trained personnel in production departments or supervisors who are not willing to wait for an engineering change notice (ECN) or the latest revision because of pressure from above to get the product out the door as scheduled.

In order to prevent unauthorized changes in the design or manufacturing processes, the changes should be controlled. Each change should be evaluated and approved by an unbiased representative of higher management. Control of all types of changes must be imposed at every level of the organization in order to assure that disastrous situations will not occur.

Change is properly done with a "document and data control" system whereby all design parameter drawings, operating procedures, material specifications, instructions, and forms must be approved by an authorized individual and disseminated to all applicable departments. When issuing revisions to existing documents it is necessary to pull previous documents from the system and verify that they have been physically destroyed. Organizations using partial or total soft-copy documents and change control releases must also validate the issuing of documents and data.

Controls on changes and new releases must be imposed and monitored for documents issued to suppliers as well. Product safety problems are commonly generated by problems in manufacturing operations as well as supplied components, assemblies, and even finished products. Documentation and data control of these activities must be a natural part of the product safety system.

CUSTOMER COMPLAINTS

The Blown Tire Issue

When we document customer complaints it is imperative that we do not introduce bias into our evaluation by automatically assuming customer wrongdoing and failing to consider manufacturing or design deficiencies. Even though some customers will fail to prove manufacturer liability and receive restitution for a product defect that could cause injury, moral and ethical issues must to be addressed by the manufacturer, particularly if that product could, by design or fabrication, cause harm to the customer.

For example, Hankook Tire, a South Korean tire manufacturer and not a household name, contracted with Ford Truck to install tires on some models of the F150 trucks. Even though the company had a fair reputation for customer satisfaction, some users of their tires questioned their quality and reliability.

Did the manufacturer have sufficient data to assure a quality and reliable product? Are tire manufacturing defects on critical characteristics less than 3.4 defective parts per million...the Six Sigma criteria? Without sufficient data to assure a quality and reliable tire, a manufacturer assumes a questionable position regarding customer safety and their tires.

It is easier and less expensive for a tire manufacturer to simply blame the customer for misuse or abuse if a tire blows while in operation. Their position is that the exploded tire was caused by a road contaminate such as a nail, a piece of glass, or a piece of sharp metal or by bad driving by the vehicle operator.

Although road contaminates and poor driving habits are not uncommon, and although they are legitimate reasons for a tire to explode and go flat, they are not the only reasons. A manufacturing defect such as bad materials, too high a process temperature in the tire mold, or too short or too long a cycle time in the process can also be logical causes of tire defects.

However, to admit that a manufacturing or design defect is a feasible cause would open up the possibility for a product recall. It is easier and significantly less expensive for the manufacturer to simply say the blown tire was caused by something other than the company's negligence. Besides, how could the end user deny that "rubber stamp" reason? What individual has enough power to dispute the tire manufacturer's explanation?

This flaw occurred in one of Hankook's truck tires and they immediately denied any responsibility for the flaw. They used such words as "heat rings" and talked about foreign matter imbedded in the tire that subsequently created an excessive weight that pushed down on the flat tire. On and on their explanation went. However, an examination by the truck dealer did not reveal any foreign matter in the tire.

While some manufacturers were preaching denial, other manufacturers were working to design and manufacture their products to better meet customer requirements, exceed regulatory or industrial standards, and support the ISO 9001 continual improvement initiative with sound and reliable data and documentation. These companies should be applauded for their commitment to preventing an injury to the end user, and society should vocally deprecate those companies that do not share this commitment.

It is no longer acceptable to simply "rubber stamp" a reason for a defect and fail to investigate the true cause of a flaw that may injure the customer. Some manufacturers mask the potential harm to the customer by claiming that their products are protected by the law under the umbrella of "limited warranty." Although limited warranty is a legitimate claim that allows for a specific limitation on the usage and application of a product, it can also be a legal way of denying responsibility.

Often there is a fine line between these two objectives. However, a good test is to determine whether the product known to cause harm to the user can be controlled by a preplanned product safety system. The system should be evaluated to assess whether these product hazard prevention activities can eliminate a failure that can harm the consumer. These activities should be done before a limited warranty condition is put in motion.

Product hazard prevention is an activity that requires a formal evaluation structure. There must be no hidden agenda of protecting the organization or downplaying the potential harm that design or manufacturing deficiencies may cause the user of the product. Once the manufacturer is satisfied that a safety assessment has been achieved and no major issues exist, it is then that a formal customer complaint system can be installed that should result in only minor deficiencies.

These assumed deficiencies should be analyzed, inspected, and tested to appraise the alleged problem. If the product is found to be nonconforming, steps must be taken to resolve the problem. There is an old adage that states, "For every complaint, there will be ten people with the same problem who will not speak out." Although this adage is challengeable, it does bring out a salient point. A customer complaint that is not taken seriously could result in a greater problem for the organization and could present the company in a poor light to existing and potential customers.

However, it is important to recognize that all customer complaints can be categorized as reactionary. That is, the situation has already occurred and now we must verify its legitimacy and then take the necessary steps to correct the problem. In most customer complaint situations the design issues have already been addressed, leaving only the manufacturing processes to be analyzed. This analysis is a pro-action initiative that should begin with the product safety council function. All manufacturing components should be reviewed to assure that sub-processes are in compliance with customer requirements and good manufacturing practices.

The council's membership must be made up of representatives who are familiar with existing manufacturing processes and who can adjust the system to add and qualify new processes that will meet the safety dimensions of the new or revised product.

However, even though a well trained product safety council can analyze the product for potential problems and go through a thorough safety hazard analysis, other safety issues may come to the surface only after the product has been tested in the real life environment. This environment can be within the organization's lab, at an independent test facility, or sometimes in the real world.

For example, let's suppose we have designed a cruise control device used for heavy vehicles and school buses. The design parameters require that we include heat-treating, metal-finishing, close-tolerance machining for specific product characteristics, and the inspection and testing of the processes in manufacturing operations. All of these functions must be sequentially incorporated in the manufacturing flow diagram in order for the finished product to meet the design criteria. This task must be conducted by a knowledgeable individual capable of determining how the stages and gates of the conceptual diagram come together. Usually this individual has the title of process engineer, project engineer, or manufacturing engineer.

The product safety council should invite this individual to sit on the council as an authority of manufacturing processes. This person's task would be to examine product safety concerns and determine whether the manufacturing process has provided for eliminating—or at least minimizing—these safety concerns.

5

Risk Management

WHAT IS RISK MANAGEMENT?

Risk is defined by the American Heritage Dictionary as "the possibility of harm or loss." *Management* is defined as "the act, manner, or practice of managing." *Managing* is to direct, control, or handle. Therefore, risk management is "the act of directing, controlling, or handling an incident that could possibly cause harm or loss to the user of the product."

There are many types of risk management scenarios. Some types include insurance policies that pay out money upon the death of the insured. Insurance companies hire actuaries to calculate the probability that the insured will live to an average age, plus or minus three standard deviations from this arithmetic mean. Previous health history is a factor as well as age, gender, and other criteria that affect the statistics of the database. All of these factors are put into a probabilistic calculation that results in a premium the company hopes is more than the payout cost plus administrative, staff support, and infrastructure cost. The result should be a profit to the insurance company, which is the ultimate objective of the organization.

The concept of risk can be carried over to automobile insurance, house insurance, and other types of insurance. But insurance is not the only risk management focus. Risk is associated with virtually every activity and every product. For example, the banking industry deals with many facets of risk related to financial services, investment banking, and loan banking. Risk associated with the recent multibillion-dollar bailouts and credit losses is an example of how critical it is that banking and security leaders monitor and manage risk involved in all economic fronts. The healthcare sector, with a wide span of patient care technologies and surgical errors, deals with another kind of risk. Perhaps the most widely recognized risk today is the risk associated with information technology and all of its ramifications.

Although there are many categories of risk management, this chapter will focus on risk management as it pertains to product safety and liability prevention. Over the years there have been a plethora of risk management approaches, analytical tools, and methods applied to this initiative. Many have failed, and many have only limited application. In general risk management is a way of managing the degree of uncertainty that exists in any organization. The initial step in the risk management process is to assess the utilization of resources that already exists in the organization. This step involves the actual operational stages of manufacturing or service processes and how those actually compare to an ideal manufacturing or service logic. After this analysis is conducted, the organization should have a better idea of the uncertainty and how to refine the processes.

The organization should concentrate on risk as the probability of an adverse happening, whether injury, peril, or even death, caused by misuse, abuse, poor design, or manufacturing defect of a product. The decision to manage risk is based on knowledge the organization has about the product being assessed. Questions arise as to whether the danger is reasonable and can be accepted with no further actions, or whether the danger is unacceptable and steps must be taken to reduce the risk.

In order to make decisions of this gravity, it's necessary to perform "risk analysis." This analysis will look at past history of the product, assessing such things as type and magnitude of failures in a specific time period. The organization must determine whether the probable loss and/or injury is justifiable for a preventive action initiative.

The organization should want to know the possible risk that may expose the company when a product enters the marketplace. BP is an example of a company that failed to install an effective risk management plan in its field operation with specific procedures and instruction policies. This failure and correction action of the oil spill in the Gulf of Mexico cost the company well over 20 billion dollars, not to mention the devastation it caused the environment. The risk manager must strive to achieve the optimum give-and-take between loss potentials due to accidents and accident prevention expenditures.

Another poorly conducted risk analysis involved the product safety review team that failed to identify and evaluate the potential harm that would be caused by an improper design of the "drop down" component of a baby crib. This design defect caused the product to be recalled by the consumer safety commission after 30 babies strangled to death in just one year. The basic premise for a risk management review is how much risk is acceptable. The answer has to do with the benefits derived from the application and the environment in which the product is used. When the risk is greater than the product safety team finds acceptable, the product is deemed unsafe and should not be released to the marketplace until the concerns are corrected.

Certain products are classified as "minimal in risk" from an effective product safety review. But regardless how minimal the product risk might be, we still must conduct a risk analysis. For example, a flashlight may seem to be low on the risk analysis scale because it would appear to cause no harm to the user. However, the product safety team analyzed the broader scope of the flashlight's application and suggested that a battery contact erroneously assembled could cause the flashlight to not light. Used in an environment such as a dark room, changing a flat tire at midnight, or in any other critical circumstances a flashlight that failed to light could cause a severe accident. Do not assume that any product might not be a candidate for potential harm to the user.

When analyzing the risk of a specific product (a baby crib, a baby's toy, an elderly person's walker, and other products that have a potential to cause harm), something that cannot be fully controlled by the user, it is important that the manufacturer use extra care in risk analysis. This may require the use of mistake proofing, error proofing, fault-tree analysis, and other such tools for the making of a safe and reliable product.

The assessment of possible risk is often a subjective analysis founded on opinion and knowledge of the product safety review team and/or the task of the risk manager. But there are many products that can incorporate the subjective analysis with empirical or classical statistics to derive a data-type base coupled with the experience and knowledge of the product and the environment in which it is exposed. Table 5.1 illustrates this assessment in a quantifiable paradigm based on severity from "one" to "ten" on a Likert Scale, accompanied by a risk assessment description and its risk level. This risk analysis scale provides the assessor with a method of determining the risk involved in the product.

Table 5.1 The risk analysis scale.

Severity	Description	Risk level
10	An accident will occur	Extremely high
9	An accident most likely will occur	Very high
8	An accident could occur	High
7	An accident might occur	Somewhat high
6	An accident is capable to occur	Moderately high
5	An accident is possible	Possibly risky
4	An accident is doubtful	Somewhat low
3	An accident is improbable	Low
2	An accident is unlikely to occur	Very low
1	An accident will not occur	Extremely low

The risk analysis scale is a tool that can be used to evaluate the gravity of a risk and the action needed to eliminate or at least reduce the possibility of accident and injury to the user. A rating of five or more requires an investigation and the documentation of action needed to change a design parameter and/or a manufacturing process.

Risk management represents a broad scope of the result of a formal risk analysis study. This analysis should indicate the potential risk to a person using the product or to persons indirectly involved with the product function. This question must be asked: "If an accident occurs, what is the probability that it will cause a minor endangerment, no injury at all, or something else up to and including a critical mishap?" Answers range from one extreme to the other, from relatively low on the risk analysis scale all the way to high, potentially involving death to the user. This risk analysis will determine the amount of time and expense an organization will invest to protect the user or someone indirectly involved with the product from harm.

A basic rule to follow is that risk appraised at five or higher on the risk analysis scale must be investigated by the product safety review team. The higher the severity ranking on the scale, the more intense the action needed to resolve the issue. All of this analysis should be carefully recorded and retained. Note: documentation control is critical to the process.

RISK MANAGEMENT – PRINCIPLES AND GUIDELINES

The following is an overview of the International Standard ISO 31000, adopted in the U.S. as ANSI/ASSE Z690.2. This standard was written as a guide to help organizations around the world recognize the value of risk management and related methodologies. Regardless of the size of the organization, some events can have an adverse influence on its performance. What we call risk is the uncertainty associated with the effects of adverse events.

Risk management is a systematic, structured, and timely approach that helps in the decision-making process and it explicitly addresses uncertainty. The nature of uncertainty and how it can be addressed should also be examined. The inputs to the process of managing risk are based on information sources such as historical data, experience, stakeholder feedback, observation, and expert judgment.

Organizations manage risk by:

a. Identifying the risk

b. Analyzing the risk

c. Evaluating whether risk severity is high enough to require corrective action

d. Reducing or eliminating the risk

These steps can be performed by a risk manager or incorporated into a product safety team's activities. Often it requires communication at all levels, both internal and external to the organization, in all four steps of the risk management process.

Risk management experts contend that the organization should manage risk as a part of its business strategic plan and change management activities, and that the risk management policy must be aligned with the organization's culture and objectives; it is not a stand-alone activity. This contention is correct and should be recognized, but without a systemic process to follow the question is this: "How effective is the risk activity?" It is, therefore, imperative that this activity not be shielded in an ancillary position within some other function; it must be in a stand-alone position or a salient part of a greater initiative such as a product safety review function.

Although risk management can be applied to all the disciplines of public and private organizations and professional associations and used for specific functions, projects, and activities, we will focus our attention on the risk involved in designing, manufacturing, and marketing a product (the product cycle).

The initial design and implementation of risk management must start with an understanding of the organization and its context. In order to cast the management risk structure we must evaluate both external and internal contexts. Once this exercise has been done and we are satisfied that we have built a platform for our risk management model, we are ready for the establishing of a risk management policy.

The risk management policy should clearly state the organization's rationale for managing risk, indicate the relationship between the organization's objectives and the policy, and assign the accountabilities and responsibilities for managing risk. In addition, the policy should express the way in which conflicting interests are handled, how human and financial resources are committed, and the method in which the organization's performances will be measured and reported. The policy should also express how it is to be reviewed from time to time, and it should be flexible enough to quickly adjust to continual improvement. All of these points should be communicated to management and staff support personnel.

Individuals who have the responsibility for specific risk functions should have the appropriate training and competence for managing risk, the accountability, and the authority to carry out their task. The individual assigned specific risk tasks should be capable of implementing and maintaining the risk management process and assuring the adequacy, effectiveness, and efficiency of any controls.

In order to ensure that risk management is effective and efficient, the organization should regularly review performance against indicators and evaluate whether the policy and the plan are still appropriate. If either is found to be not effective, a decision should be made to improve these criteria.

Although risk management covers a broad area of the organizational structure, we will address only the product liability prevention facet of it. The basic concept of the "risk" subset is to construct the model as a process control approach. This will be designed in the form of the process paradigm: input, transformation, and output. The basic premise of risk management, as it is applied specifically to product liability prevention, is that risk is characterized by the effect of potential events and the consequences of those events. Events can lead to a range of consequences with either positive or negative effects. We will study primarily the negative effects pertaining to product safety and the likelihood that something will happen.

The first step in the risk management process is the development of a communication and consultation plan. This step should address concerns relating to the risk itself, its cause, its consequences, and the measures being taken to treat the concern. The consultative team members can be a stand-alone group or part of the product safety review function; the product safety team members can represent both functions.

Some of the activities of the consultative team are to help establish the context, help ensure that risks are adequately identified, bring team members' expertise together for analyzing and evaluating risk, and secure management's endorsement and support for a treatment plan. The communication and consultation plan must take into account that its holistic responsibility is to participate in all the other activities of the risk management process in a bilateral mode.

After the organization has established the plan (the input of the process) the next step (the transformation of the process) is to establish the context. The context primarily sets the scope and risk criteria for the remaining processes. It looks at both internal and external parameters. External parameters that focus on product safety criteria include the application of the product and any misuse or abuse of the product. This plan would also examine the potential for foreseeable or unforeseeable conditions that might cause harm to the user of the product.

Internal parameters focus on design and manufacturing product safety issues. Design issues are derived from poor design practices, a design that fails to recognize a potential condition that might cause injury or peril to the user, and poor manufacturing practices that would result in unsafe conditions. Poor manufacturing may be caused by untrained operators making mistakes, production supervisors cutting operating expenses, the lack of good manufacturing equipment and processes in meeting the tolerance criteria, or simply the lack of effective operating procedures and instructions.

In addition to design and manufacturing parameters that are performed incorrectly, other ancillary functions such as poor quality assurance practices, insufficient materials management, improper manu-facturing engineering, and a poor preventive maintenance program also affect product safety. Any of these internal stakeholder disciplines can have an adverse effect on the safety factors of a product.

In the context structure the organization should define criteria to be used to evaluate the significance of risk. Criteria can be derived from legal and regulatory requirements, customer requirements, and/or industrial standards. Both the risk management policy and the plan should be developed and the process should be continually reviewed. Responsible individuals should assess such factors as the nature and types of causes and consequences that can occur and how they will be measured, how likely it is that they might occur, and the level of risk involved. This process is called risk assessment.

RISK ASSESSMENT IN THE PRODUCT CYCLE

After the context activity has been complete the organization should start the process of risk assessment. Risk assessment is the overall process of risk identification, risk analysis, and risk evaluation. The risk assessment activity is the umbrella under which the subcomponents are structured. For specific guidance in risk assessment technique, see the ISO/IEC 31010 document.

The first step in the risk assessment process is risk identification (the transformation stage). The aim of this step is to generate a broad list of risks based on occurrences that might produce the restriction or the attainment of objectives. All risk must be identified regardless of whether it appears to be significant to an opportunity, or whether it is identified to be included in further analysis studies.

Risk source can be internal or external to the organization and all risk should be identified. The organization must establish a plan to identify the source of the risk. The plan should consider the consequences of risk, identify what might happen, and consider all possible causes and scenarios that show potential consequences. Employees with appropriate knowledge should be involved in identifying risks and should be called upon to assist in the risk identification process.

The second step in the risk assessment process is risk analysis. This step involves developing an understanding of the risk. It entails investigation into the causes and sources of risk, the pros and cons of risk consequences, and the probability that those consequences will occur. The manufacturer should identify the factors that affect consequences and their possibility of occurrence.

If an organization has existing risk controls, their effectiveness and efficiency should be verified. An event can have more than one consequence and can affect more than one objective, so the analysis activity must consider the interdependence of different risks and their sources.

Risk analysis can be very detailed in structure or relatively simple. Risk analysis can use high-level statistics or it can use non-statistical tools for analysis modeling. The risk analysis depends primarily on the risk event and the purpose of the analysis and the information that is available.

Results can be conveyed in terms of tangible and intangible impacts. Once the analysis has been conducted, it may reflect a multi-level risk and its sensitivity to presumptions, suppositions, and postulations that are formed by the risk analysis activity; this should be considered in the analysis process.

The third and last step of the risk assessment process is risk evaluation. The purpose of this step is to assist in making a decision about the potential risk involved in the manufacturing of a product. The evaluation is based on the results of the risk analysis, consideration of which risk is in need of treatment, and the method and priority for the implementation of the treatment.

A decision to determine the risk action should be made based on the magnitude of the risk, the resulting harm of the risk, and compliance with all governmental, regulatory, and professional society standards and customer requirements. The risk evaluation can result in a decision not to conduct a risk treatment, but to continue with the existing controls. The evaluation may reveal the need to undertake further analysis.

The decision to treat risk is based, oftentimes, not on a set plan but rather on the present goals and objectives of the organization. Manufacturers that have an established risk plan might have elected to use the culture, attitude, and risk criteria as their baseline for the risk decision.

RISK TREATMENT IN THE PRODUCT CYCLE

After a detailed risk assessment has been conducted, a decision must be made by the risk management team to determine whether a risk treatment is needed. If the decision is to do nothing, the risk assessment process must be documented; records of the assessment actions must be retained for the life of the product. If the risk assessment process determined that a risk treatment is to be initiated, a risk treatment action must be implemented.

Risk treatment in the manufacturing sector is basically a modification to an existing risk management plan. The primary reason for a risk treatment is to strengthen the plan's effectiveness or minimize the probability that a risk endangerment may result in harm to the end user in a product safety action.

There are several risk treatment choices that are independent of each other. For example, one option is to eschew the risk by electing not to begin or continue with the risk activity, or simply removing the risk source. Other options would be to change the consequences or likelihood of the risk.

SELECTION OF THE RISK TREATMENT PLAN

Choosing the most suitable risk treatment is a conjoined resolution between the financial resources the organization is willing to spend and the cost of doing nothing to minimize the risk. Sometimes it is difficult to assess whether the cost of implementation will derive benefits that justify the efforts. Integrated into this decision is the perception that the organization is being a "good neighbor" and complying with social responsibility, meeting regulatory and other requirements, and protecting the natural environment.

The risk treatment plan should be designed to assess which risk can justify treatment, regardless of whether it is justified on an economical basis. Risk treatment should be evaluated on its merit. For example, if the consequence is high (severe) and the likelihood of the risk is low (infrequent), the treatment may differ from a converse example. The risk treatment plan should include a matrix of this assessment.

The risk treatment process may uncover other risk factors that also must be assessed and treated. These new risk factors should be handled in the same manner as the original risk and incorporated into the same process, not treated as a new risk. This connection between the original risk and the new risk should be emphasized and maintained.

Developing and Executing the Risk Treatment Plan

The intention of a risk treatment plan is to document the implementation process of the risk concern. Risk criteria include the expected benefits derived from the plan, proposed treatment actions, resources required, performance measures and constraints, reporting and monitoring controls, and the timetable from start to finish of the process.

The plan should be designed to identify the executive management people accountable for the execution of it and those individuals who are responsible for its implementation. The risk treatment plan should be incorporated into the manufacturing processes and the organization's culture and communicated with all "owners" of the proposed plan's actions.

Executive management should be cognizant of residual risk. Residual risk (also referred to as "retained risk") is risk that remains after a risk treatment; it can contain unidentified risk. This residual risk should be a part of the documentation and monitoring process and should be subject to critiquing and further treatment, where needed.

Risk Treatment Monitoring and Critiquing

After risk treatment has been implemented, a monitoring function and, where needed, a critiquing function should be conducted. These activities can be carried out on a cyclic basis by an assigned risk management team or an *ad hoc* committee formed for this specific activity.

This activity should be clearly defined and should include all aspects of the risk management framework. Its purpose is to ensure that the controls are effective and efficient, and to procure additional information to improve the risk assessment process. The monitoring and critique stage encompasses the analyzing of risk treatment trends, its successes, its failures, and any changes to the risk criteria. The monitoring activity can also identify any looming risks.

The results of monitoring should be recorded and should be used as an information source for any salient issues to the risk treatment critique function. Records provide the foundation for improvement in manufacturing functions and processes. Good record keeping allows the organization to analyze information at a later date or for other risk treatment projects. This recording element is a critical aspect of the product safety and product liability prevention process and can play a key role in any potential litigation.

Risk, in its holistic scope, has many functions. It connotes the uncertainty of an event's effect on other objectives. If we can manage risk, we can better assess the probability that a negative event will occur. In the function of product safety and product liability prevention, we should not delete the risk management function from these product analysis initiatives.

6

Product Recall Guidelines

Product recall is a reactionary action that happens when a product defect causes injury or impairs the function of the product to the user. Reactionary action occurs because we know after the product has been produced that there was noncompliance in either design, systems, or manufacturing that resulted in a defect. The best way to avoid exposing an organization to a recall is to minimize the conditions that would exhibit a product defect.

Anyone who has been subject to a recall knows that it can be expensive and traumatizing to an organization and to the user of the product. The organization has a responsibility to remove the product from circulation as soon as possible to prevent damage or harm. Each day the product is in the field there is greater probability of injury to the user or potential costly down time to a customer. Customers will be forced to stop using the product because of the subsequent harm it may cause, so it is to everyone's benefit that the recall be done expeditiously and economically. In all cases the manufacturer bears the cost of the recall, and removing the defective product from the market or correcting it as soon as possible will reduce that cost and reduce the likelihood of compensable injury to the user.

Manufacturers know that product safety should be one of their most critical goals, yet even with this awareness, many do not have a plan to address this question: "What happens if a defect is found in the field?" Some of the most obvious causes of a product liability situation are defective materials, improper design, manufacturing nonconformities, and failure to properly warn the user of hazards. All of these reasons must be addressed in a preventive mode to minimize customer exposure to unsafe products that have entered the marketplace and can subsequently be subject to a product recall.

The recall of a product is generally a management decision. It is not necessary for the product to have already been involved in a casualty and to have caused harm before a recall action can be implemented. It's only necessary that the product have a defect that could result in an accident or malfunction before the organization can command an action. The exception is when a recall is mandated by a government agency. A recall can be for the purpose of destroying, replacing, or altering the product. A recall is made to protect the user of the product, but it also protects the manufacturer from additional judicial efforts that could be initiated by the user to redress for damages.

The performance of a recall procedure requires manpower and financial resources. The recall is likely to be more successful and less expensive if a plan and a traceability system exist.

RECALL PLANNING PROCEDURE

The recall planning procedure can be incorporated into the quality management system as part of the document control subsystem. This function is oftentimes assigned to the quality assurance head or to his or her delegate as the product recall coordinator. Whether the head of quality or someone else in the organization is assigned the coordinator's responsibility, the function should be assigned to an individual who is empowered to quarterback the function.

The product recall procedure functions as a guide, providing staff and line personnel an organization framework within which to work and a method for describing the responsibility of each person.

Although there may be other objectives set forth in a procedure, the main decisions to delineate are the following:

a. Who is to conduct the recall and who will perform which tasks during the recall.

b. How to protect the customer, user, bystander, and company.

c. How the company will assure compliance with the various laws and government regulations.

d. How to remove, upgrade, or repair unacceptable or questionable products from the marketplace at minimum cost and with minimum inconvenience to the customer.

e. How to protect the assets of the company.

The procedure should be written to state the main objectives of the recall. The plan should also direct those individuals involved to:

1. Specifically identify the product involved.

2. Clearly differentiate between product that is being recalled and product that is not subject to recall, repair, or replacement.

3. Identify the location of product to be recalled.

4. Stop the manufacturing and further distribution of defective product.

5. Isolate, correct, or dispose of nonconforming product(s).

6. Be prepared with a plan for how a specific product would be recalled prior to an actual recall.

7. Identify who will do what within an organized response to recall events.

8. Adjust the product development and manufacturing system to preclude a recurrence of the problem, within acceptable economic and technical limitations.

9. Obtain a clear understanding of the various activities and outline the operation and the duties of the various individuals involved in the activity.

10. Prevent further damage to the organization.

A careful definition of the decision and of who is to perform each of the activities will result in a timely response to the problem, protection of the customers, and a minimization of expenditures. The planning must provide for a system to identify where various products are shipped and, if possible, their present location. An important part of the procedure is the definition of responsibility: responsibility for preparing a system and responsibility for operating a recall.

The recall plan must specifically define the role that each individual and group will play in the organization. The plan must also develop the system to fit the particular corporate environment so that action, when needed, can occur promptly, efficiently, and logically.

There are two essential elements of the recall task: a leader with a staff and a recall procedure. The leader and staff should be selected from those who are already familiar with the product. They will be best able to answer questions about the product and deal effectively with users and others who will need to know how to handle returns or on-site repair.

The second element needed is a recall procedure that is as specific as possible. One of the best ways to minimize the extent of a recall is to be able to identify the exact products that must be recalled. With large items that are identified by serial numbers, this will be easier if careful records are kept that identify components and parts used. Other methods include the marking of components with bar codes or identification marks indicating lot size, time and date of manufacturing, material heat number or batch numbers, and any other data that would be significant for capturing the defective product.

In developing a recall procedure each organization must tailor its specific needs in detail. Often this means different procedures for different products produced by the same company. Consequently, the recall procedure and records for these products can be dissimilar.

The recall procedure should identify assigned individuals and outline step-by-step instructions for such processes as news releases and notification to owners, users, and distributors of the product. It also should cover, where applicable, correction and repair notices, government agencies to be notified, check lists of each step to be performed and who is to do it, and how items in the field are to be identified and located.

ORGANIZATION RECALL FINANCES

A second task critical to providing management with a framework for a product recall is the development of "time and expense" rules and their appropriate accounts. A method is needed to capture the costs involved in a recall and allocate the costs to the proper functions in the organization. The recall cost should include administration services, notification cost, cost of goods manufactured (material, labor, packaging, and so on), the cost of travel time and expenses to coordinate the recall, return shipping, on-site repairs, physical scrapping of products, and other ancillary costs (legal fees, insurance cost, temporary help, engineering design changes, production tooling modifications, image control, and so on).

These costs should be estimated at the planning stage. If a recall occurs, costs should be tracked as the recall proceeds and accounts revised as needed. The cost accounting function should be administered to show feedback on what has been spent and how that compares to the estimated cost and how the accomplishment and time status of the recall relates to the projection.

A product recall usually draws on in-house disciplines such as engineering, quality assurance, material management, marketing, and so on. It is important that the recall cost not be assigned to any entity without their knowledge of the expenses and the reason behind them.

Product recall costs are overhead costs that continue to be incurred throughout the length of the recall project. Proper tracking and monitoring are critical to the realization of total cost and the proper accounting disposition of the monies spent. Management costs must also be built into the financial framework for recall, including legal and executive costs at the various levels of the organization that have contributed to the design of the recall and are involved as decision makers on issues that arise.

Sometimes insurance costs are affected. The insurer may demand increases to expedite the return and recovery of recalled product. Insurance cost can be vulnerable to the exposure an organization faces during a product recall and to the company's failure to have a plan in place to capture product in the field. The consequence of not having an effective recall process can be increases in insurance cost or termination of the policy altogether.

One of the major elements of a product recall is the notification process, which is classified according to the seriousness of the problem. Products determined to be critical because of potential for harm require a more comprehensive recall campaign. This campaign may require notification that involves the media, government agencies, and a formal communication mode to all users. Recall of a product that is not likely to harm the end user and that, at most, will cause inconvenience or shorter functional life, requires a limited program of well-designed notices to customers or distributors and may be sufficient to discharge reasonable notification efforts.

Notification efforts must be designed to communicate three things clearly and in a visually acceptable manner: that a recall is being conducted, what the hazard is, and how to deal with the defective product. As the recall progresses, the manufacturer should evaluate which notification tools have been most and least cost effective in reaching and influencing product users. These evaluations should be taken into account in design of subsequent notification efforts.

IDENTIFICATION AND TRACEABILITY (I&T)

A product recall is the result of something gone wrong in the manufacturing of a product that would subsequently cause harm to the user of that product. This issue is so important that the International Organization of Standardizations (ISO) addresses it in specific documents of ISO 9001 and ISO 9004 under the subheading Identification and Traceability.

In order for a recall to be effective, it's necessary to establish a method to identify the product and its critical components. Once this is done, it's necessary to develop a system to trace the product throughout its life cycle.

Essentially ISO 9001 is a process-based quality management system that guides manufacturers and service organizations in the collection of data and the establishment of effective systems. Identification and Traceability requires the producer of the product to develop a process for data collection that can be used for product improvement and recall capability. In this chapter we will focus on the recall capability.

According to ISO 9001, the requirement of I&T is this:

Where appropriate, the organization shall identify the product by suitable means throughout product realization. The organization shall identify the product status with respect to monitoring and measurement requirements. Where traceability is a requirement, the organization shall control and record the unique identification of the product.

In short, the purpose of I&T is to mitigate the use of defective product. The first objective of I&T is to create a system for identifying all critical components of the product. For example, consider a product that exhibited a stress crack in the field that could cause the part to fail and harm the user. You have been notified by the customer that a failure has occurred on equipment in which your product is attached.

The first step is to validate the failure. This can be done by requesting a sample of the product be returned to you for evaluation. Depending on the magnitude of potential harm to the user, you may want to visit the customer or failure site immediately. Once you have made a comprehensive evaluation and determined the stress crack is due to a failure in your manufacturing processes, it is imperative to drill down in the process to determine the root cause.

Assuming that the problem is due to a failure of steel purchased from your supplier, you would need to make use of your previously developed system for capturing the "heat number" of the steel mill that produced the heat of steel. This number must be forwarded along with your production routing to each actual part produced or the lot size of that order. This can be done by inscribing each part with an identification number traceable to the heat number, or by cross-referencing the heat number and any other significant process on the part or paperwork attached to the customer's order.

This lot number or batch number must also be traceable to the dates of production and shipping. If internal records do not indicate which dated products used the stress crack parts and there is no way to identify the defective group by sight, the customer would have to return all the items produced and the factory would have to replace all the parts. If the product is to be repaired in the field, all would have to be repaired.

It is essential to know the cause of the product failure and to have good record data, but it is equally important to be able to identify where the recalled product actually was sold and who is the user or owner of that product. Therefore, a system should be in place to account for all customers that may be exposed to the defective product. One way to accomplish this task is to program and sort all critical and special processes and suppliers. Raw materials should be traceable to shipping data and part identity, if possible. On some high-quantity items it is difficult to keep track of where each item was sold and to whom it was sold. The only way to identify where high-quantity parts are sold is through advertisements, radio, news, television, and similar announcements.

This action can be significantly expensive if the I&T is not properly instituted, so it is advantageous to the company to take the time to develop an effective and efficient system. The more exact the product record keeping, the better the probability of reducing the recall cost and the less chance of a product liability lawsuit. It only takes one part that is not captured to cause a product lawsuit.

Most government agencies require prompt notification of a recall when the risk of harm to the user is severe or an unreasonable number of failures have occurred. The quick conclusion of the recall process, with a high capture rate, means the overall cost will be less and likelihood of litigation will be less. It's important to expedite a recall, but it's equally important to capture as many defective parts as possible.

If the recall is a manufacturer process problem, then product may be identified in the field by product codes, lot numbers, and dates. If the defect is a design safety problem, then model, revision, and serial numbers may be important factors. In most cases, one method or the other can capture all or most of the defective parts. However, in many industries the manufacturer has no knowledge of where a product ends up. It's necessary to rely on the distributor or seller, which makes the recall more difficult. Therefore, it is essential that the distributor or seller's internal recall system be substantiated and confirmed.

Some large complex items must be corrected or rectified in the field. It's logical and economical to send a technician into the field to correct the defective product. In the automotive industry, where product is located in many places, it may be more economical and effective for the manufacturer to provide an external service center with a specific identification system and detailed instruction on how to correct the defective product.

Product recalls are easier if the time is short between the date of receipt in the field and notification of the recall, particularly if the product life and shelf life are short (for example, foods, drugs, beverages, cosmetics, organics, and other biochemical products). However, many products have a longer product life that can effectively exceed their shelf life (for example, rubber, plastics, and metal products), and can be useful even beyond their recommended operating life. This becomes an important consideration in a traceability plan.

The longer the product life, the greater the numbers of similar items likely to be present in the distribution chain and in the hands of the user. Over a period of time, it may be impossible to determine which design or process revisions have been incorporated in specific lot sizes. Therefore, it is critical to the recall process that the organization establishes an effective plan to control all design and process revisions in the document and data control system. Likewise, it is imperative that the company have a record keeping subsystem that provides for a longer-lived product. The record retention element of your quality management system must be designed to be salient to your product recall process.

Inspection and testing should be performed on the product at various stages in the manufacturing process and records should be kept at all steps of the operation. These evaluations should be conducted before and after any design changes and they should be formalized, signed by an authorized individual in the organization, and dated. This data should be traceable to the product at shipping by a serial number, date of shipment, or lot size identification.

The better the bridge of data retention and good record keeping, the better the "bookbinding" of the products being recalled and the less cost incurred by the company. When a recall is initiated, the company must be able to tap into a previously developed system that identifies where specific shipments were sent and through what system they were distributed. This initiative will greatly simplify a product recall and control the recall cost.

The retention of records, how long to keep documents and data, is discretionary and subject to the policies and objectives of the company. There is no standard retention period that is accepted by all product liability experts, and each state has its own retention requirements. However, for the purpose of providing objective evidence that the organization intended to design and produce a safe product with a reasonable assurance that no harm would come to the end user, the following is recommended:

- Design documents and data: life of the product

- Manufacturing processes: minimum of five years

- Supplier records of inspection and test: minimum of five years

- Internal inspection and test data: minimum of five years

- Warranty and return goods assessments: minimum of five years

- All other documents and data: minimum of one year

This liability calendar is only a guide; organizations are responsible for their own record retention durations and can be guided by the statute of limitations for their particular products and state requirements in effect for each manufacturing facility. For manufacturers outside of the United States the same criteria apply.

Once you have developed a product recall plan and have initiated an effective product recall system, it is recommended that you conduct a trial run. This trial run should evaluate product safety review activities, the identification and traceability criteria, and the results of an effective product process including a sound record keeping of the salient functions. This trial run should randomly select a specific lot that was actually shipped to a multitude of customers. This product would have been verified to conform to specifications, and would have been subject to the capture of defective products from multi-location as well as multi-customer shipments.

This test would simulate a real recall situation and would validate the recall's effectiveness. If the trial run is found to have weak areas, flaws can be corrected and the product recall plan modified.

A recall is expensive and can actually destroy a company if not properly performed, but failing to develop a product recall system exposes the organization to potential disaster. The manufacturer has a responsibility to remove the product from circulation and to use a tested recall system to prevent damage and injury to the end users of the product. Every organization must evaluate its own situation and the potential need for improvement to retrieve more products. It is in the company's best interest to initiate a product recall system to protect the public from harm or loss and for its own protection against the possibility of litigation.

DAMAGE CONTROL

The whole idea of "making of a safe product" is to prevent harm or peril to the user. Virtually everything we have addressed in this book promotes the objective of preventing a defect that might cause harm or loss to the end user. This proactive approach has been the baseline for minimizing risk to the manufacturer and safeguarding the user. However, some situations slip through the preventing action and subsequently result in a product recall.

When a product recall takes place it opens the company's image to public exposure. This negative exposure can be devastating to the manufacturer if not controlled. One way to reduce this effect is to apply damage control. Damage control can be defined as "a method of communication by words and action that will strive to nullify, or at least minimize, the damage to the company's image."

Many larger organizations employ a full-time person who is responsible for external publicity. This person is usually talented in saying or doing the right thing to change the company's image or perception to the outside world. For example, Toyota had a major problem with acceleration on some vehicles. Allegedly, it would stick and cause the vehicle to speed up, a condition that could subsequently cause harm or death to the driver of that vehicle. In addition to this problem, Toyota had several other vehicle recalls in their family of automobiles. Shortly after the news media publicized Toyota's acceleration incidents, Toyota's manager of public relations quarterbacked an advertising campaign that promoted many safety awards the company had received in the recent past. The company did not mention in its advertisement any assumed defect that could impair the safety of passengers of these vehicles, but rather presented a "red herring" fallacy of relevance suggesting the product is assumed to be safe.

This red herring stratagem most likely did exculpate the company's image to many potential and existing owners of Toyota vehicles; it could, in fact, positively influence the company's future sales, but it is still a marketing contrivance. However, the company risks that the public will see through this strategy. That is to say, customers will know that just because the company received previous safety awards, it doesn't mean the company will always produce a safe vehicle.

Damage control is a sensitive function and can work for or against an organization. Many smaller companies do not have the funds to employ a full-time manager of public relations and must rely on a public relations consulting firm to represent their public image in the case of a product recall or other negative situation. But regardless of the size of the organization, how a company handles a recall affects its image, its financial position, and its ability to survive.

An important part of damage control is the deployment of an ad hoc committee responsible for reviewing the final actions prior to the actual public notice and advertisement strategies. This committee should comprise executive heads from quality assurance, sales, manufacturing, design engineering, and administrated management (executive vice president, vice president of operations, or the equivalent).

This group should also participate in a product recall final acceptance. The product recall coordinator should present a final action plan and the step-by-step process that will be employed for the recall and secure approval sign-off and any recommended suggestions from the group. The group must be in 100% agreement before implementation is begun for product recall and damage control activities.

There are product recalls going on as you read this chapter. Basically this is due to two reasons. It's sometimes simply impossible to guarantee that no harm will befall the user of a product in all situations; any product can, by product design, be dangerous if misused or carelessly used (for example, a knife or chain saw). Other factors as a matter of chance and circumstances can cause a product to fail (a severe windstorm causes the electricity to go off or an ice storm causes a car to slide off the road). There is probably no single product that is totally free of potential to cause harm or loss to the user. We cannot design a product that would be intrinsically evaluated to be unimpeded from somehow causing harm or loss to the user of that product. That's why it is essential to have a product recall system in place before its needed.

The second reason for product recall is the organization's failure to develop a product safety function that can be integrated into its existing structure. This book outlines how this can be done in the most economical way, but not to the cost of missing or omitting key elements in the making of a safe product. However, justifiable as this reason is, it does take a commitment and involvement from top management to develop this function. This initiative may prevent the need for a product recall.

7

Reliability Systems

Every product has some kind of function, and some products are more complex and have more utility than others. Even a pet rock has a function. It can be perceived as a "good luck" charm that provides the owner a feeling of compassion and caring. In the broader scope, it does have a function...physiologically speaking and regardless how silly it may sound. But when we think more pragmatically we think in terms of a product's reliability to function time and time again (for example, a light switch, a cell phone, an ink pen, a television, an automobile, and so on).

In this chapter we will discuss the basic parameters of reliability and the general techniques that can be applied to virtually every functional item (but we will use a more complicated example than a pet rock).

The ultimate objective of any product is to perform in a decisive manner all the time, resulting in the intended output of that specific function. In order to assure that this objective is met, we establish a reliability system structured to meet this purpose.

The term that we will used to describe the overall capability of a product to accomplish its purpose is "product effectiveness." Essentially, if the product is effective, it will function properly over a given period of time and under normal conditions. If the product is not effective, the manufacturer must investigate the reason for the ineffectiveness and resolve this deficiency.

A reliability system starts at the time of the "fuzzy front end," when the product is in the inception of its development. At this stage the proposed product is studied for its design parameters and features that will make it withstand environmental extremes and any potential misuse and abuse. Concerns about the feasibility of the product design should be addressed at this time. It is advisable to gather as much knowledge of the design concept as possible—finite element analysis (FEA) for possible stress fractures, design failure mode and effect analysis (DFMEA), fault tree analysis (FTA), fish bone analysis, as well as other key analytical tools that can be applied to make the product as reliable as possible.

At this early stage it is quite possible the company won't have the tools or the information needed to properly assess the total effects of the product in a working environment; this is certainly not the time to establish an analysis process. It is time, however, to begin to study the effects of the product in the environment in which it will be used. One of the biggest mistakes many companies make is to settle for information derived at this stage to determine the reliability of the product.

The second step in developing sound data for your reliability system is in the pre-production stage. In this stage the quality and engineering departments review product specifications and application criteria and assess the amount of testing and inspection needed to assure that the product will be reliable and safe to the end user. In this stage the company will conduct a program of simulated environmental testing to determine whether the product will be reliable in application. This data will be recorded and modifications to the reliability testing will be made if needed to meet or improve the effectiveness of the reliability system.

The objective of this reliability testing is to validate the performance and safety while the product is functioning in the hands of a user. At these early stages in the product development process, it is possible that the initial design might be incapable of functioning as intended if it is moved from the reliability testing lab and subjected to a more severe condition in the actual usage environment. Therefore, it is essential that all functional and design concerns be resolved and the appropriate changes be incorporated and verified.

The next objective is to evaluate manufacturing processes to assure that the product is meeting dimensional and attribute requirements and that it has passed all testing prerequisites. In this production stage the organization will want to closely analyze complaints from the field and resolve reliability issues and any safety concerns. Most reliability issues and safety concerns should have been addressed before production processes begin. Ideally this action should take place immediately after the feasibility study. This is done primarily because some problems can be eliminated before they become bigger problems and can be resolved more easily and more economically prior to production.

The last step of the reliability system is the post-production stage. This stage is designed to assure that a product is reliable in the field and will function as intended without subjecting the end user to harm or loss. At this time "the horse is out of the barn and running down the hill." We have moved from a proactive mode to a reactive mode that can expose the company to a product recall condition. It is essential that we respond quickly to reliability complaints or warnings from the customer that a problem might exist involving our product.

Reliability has been defined as the probability that a system will perform satisfactorily for at least a specific period of time when used under stated conditions. The operative word is *probability*. Probability is a statistic somewhere between absolute certainty and absolute impossibility (1 & 0). For example, an average 60-watt electric light bulb is designed to light for approximately 760 hours, plus or minus three standard deviations from the arithmetic mean. If the deviation has been calculated to be 20 hours, then 99.73% of the time the light bulb will function between 700 and 820 hours.

The reliability lab may select, at random, 100 light bulbs from each day's production lot and conduct a life test and record the time to failure for each sample piece. An ongoing control calculation of the data range will be compared to the upper and lower control limits to determine the scope of a reliable light bulb. If the light bulb's life is greater than 820 hours, then the customer is getting a longer life and the bulb meets and exceeds the reliability requirement. Any light bulb life that is equal to or greater than 700 hours would meet the reliability requirement. But if the light bulb failed before 700 hours of usage, then a non-conformance in the reliability system exists and an investigation into the condition should be conducted.

This example typifies any product testing parameter for virtually all types of products. But many products are not as defined in the reliability criteria that we used for this example. A reliability system must consider many testing parameters. Some concepts associated with the reliability system's effectiveness are as follows:

- *Operational readiness* – the probability that the system is either operating satisfactorily or ready to be placed in operation on demand when used under stated conditions

- *Maintainability* – the probability that, when maintenance action is initiated under stated conditions, a failed system will be restored to operable condition within a specified total down time

- *Repairability* – the probability that a failure system will be restored to operable condition within a specified active repair time

- *Serviceability* – the degree of ease or difficulty with which a system can be repaired

In the study of reliability the salient focus is on the understanding of statistics and specifically the probability of a failure or the probability that the product will function each and every time. A single-purpose product is one that depends on only one function to meet the customer's requirements. For example, a clock is designed to give only the time of day, without any other features. If we were to add other functions to the clock, such as a dynamite actuator with a safety-warning signal used in the mining industry, our device would be classified as a multi-functional product.

In our single-purpose products the clock either indicated the time or did not. The clock either functions or does not function correctly. If it functions correctly it will show the correct time. If it does not function correctly it will either not work at all or it will indicate an erroneous time (too fast or too slow). When a product safety review team reviews the function of a clock, they might assess the possible harm to the user of the clock at a nominal risk at most. If the clock does not work properly it might make the user too early or too late for an engagement, but most likely it will not cause them harm or peril.

The reliability system for a clock may be less stringent than for an explosive device. It may only require that each clock pass through a time signal test to indicate the clock is working and that the time is accurate to some known standard. The results of the 100% testing are recorded; if too many clocks are in non-compliance to the testing standard, an action to resolve the problem is undertaken. In this case the reliability system is relatively simple and does not require the product safety review team to be an active committee after the initial review. The probability of failure after the product is in the marketplace is very small, and it is unlikely that the product will cause harm or peril to the user. Consequently, the likelihood of a product recall is slim.

This question might be asked. Should a manufacturer still have a product safety review of this type of product? The answer is "yes." Any new or existing product that does not have a sound product safety review program in place, and has not incorporated the review directly into the reliability system, subjects the organization to product safety issues and a possible product recall and product liability lawsuits. The company must think in a proactive rather than a reactive mode to minimize potential risk.

We have assessed the clock as something not likely to cause harm or peril to the end user; there is no indication that misuse or abuse of the product would be harmful to the user, and there are no unforeseeable dangers to consider. Many products fall into this category.

The multi-purpose explosive device, used in the mining industry to clear coal, salt, copper, and so on from the ground, is an excellent example. The product is initially assembled so that the timing device is integrated into the explosive sensor to activate the dynamite with a preset signal that audibly warns employees working in the area that an explosion is about to occur.

This product is dependent on all three subsystems to work in concert in order to properly perform the intended function. If any of the subsystems fails, the result could cause harm or peril to the users of the product and bystanders. For example, in the first event of the explosive device, it is critical that the clock indicate the right time the explosive will be detonated.

If the time is off by even a couple of seconds, it could cause harm or peril to the people in the surrounding area.

The second event is the warning component, an alarm signal that goes off a minute or so before the explosion to warn the people in the area of an impending explosion. This signaling device must perform at 100% reliability. A failure to operate, or a missed time signal, could cause harm or peril to individuals in the area. The last function is the actual activation of the explosive device. Once the exact time of the explosion has been decided and once the warning signal has been conducted, it is time to activate the device. It must activate with a 100% reliability or possible harm or peril to the surrounding people can result.

Regardless of whether the product is a single-functional or a multi-function item, it must be assessed for its reliability system and the effects a malfunction might cause to the end user. Regardless of whether something is a stand-alone product or a component of another product, it must be evaluated for the severity of the consequences of a failure to function properly. If a product safety team determines potential failure to be a high-risk characteristic that may cause harm or peril to the end user, it may be necessary to incorporate a "redundancy system" into the design parameter. This is subsequently reviewed by the product safety review.

The product safety review team must be capable of visualizing possible situations that might cause the product to fail or malfunction when exposed to uncertain conditions. This team must be trained to think in a proactive mode rather than a reactive mode, and they must be aware of possible environmental circumstances that may contribute to a product flaw.

Several reliability techniques can be applied to determine overall reliability system composites. *Reliability allocations* are the process of assigning reliability requirements to individual levels of the system to attain the desired system reliability. *Feasibility predictions* are the initial estimate of the feasibility of developing an operational reliability. Although these methods are helpful in the design of a reliability system, they will not be included in this text. They are too detailed and may require a higher level of reliability training. But abstractly we will abridge these two reliability techniques.

Reliability allocation focuses on the interactions between and among components, subsystems, and system reliability, resulting in a better understanding of the potential problems inherent in the product design. Reliability allocation technique could lead to optimum system reliability, since this activity would provide for such factors as corrective maintenance, basic product cost, stress factors, and other application criteria. The allocation process requires a mutual acceptance by the customer and the ultimate user of the product and is subject to ongoing product refinements. Original design parameters should be critically examined and revised as more product knowledge is obtained.

Feasibility prediction focuses on design concepts and estimated complexity. A review of the environmental accomplishments of similar systems can be of benefit in evaluating the significance of the reliability problem, which confronts the proposed new product. Complexity is measured in terms of the number of active element groups (AEG) comprising the system.

REDUNDANCY

Redundancy can be defined as a system that has more than one path to fulfill a desired result. What this means is that all subsystem components must fail in a parallel or series design before the system will not function. The basic concept of a redundant system is that failure of a redundant path will not necessarily result in a system failure. This duplication of functional components provides protection that if failure occurs in one path of operation the system can still function correctly if another path performs without failure. The criticality of the product function, the cost of a failure in injury to a person, or the high cost due to a product failure will oftentimes dictate the number of redundancy paths in the design stages.

There are two basic redundancy categories, the primary path and the secondary path. When the primary system does not function, a secondary system will kick in. The most common example is the electric system in a building. If the electricity goes off for any reason, a back-up generator, running on gas or propane, will activate. In this situation another secondary system, charged by a high-powered battery, will be activated if the gas or propane generator fails.

There are many situations in which redundancy plays a key part in the overall reliability system activity. For example, let us consider a cruise ship designed to transport customers from point "A" to point "B" and beyond. It is also designed to have subsystems such as many types of foods available, scheduled entertainments, physical and fun activities, and a comfortable and safe living and play environment. Each subsystem must work independently and in concert with all the others. Some will require back-up paths both in series and in parallel subsystems in case of subsystem failure.

If one of the several engines of the ship malfunctions, the other engines will keep the ship on course and moving. The ship will not stop in deep water and create panic in the passengers. Each and every subsystem must be examined and reviewed for its reliability to all others and from within its own functions. For example, if the chef becomes ill one morning and cannot perform the normal duties, is there a back-up chef who can step in? If the main entertainer of the evening show becomes ill, can the ship's management provide a back-up entertainer? In other words, all components should be subject to a contingency plan.

Series configuration is basic and simple; it is a system that requires the first function to perform without failure before the second and subsequent functions occur. Any system malfunction in the sequential process will shut down the intended purpose.

Parallel configuration is a basic multi-path function that requires only one of two or more subsystems running in parallel to each to result in a successful outcome. Essentially, operation "A," the first step, must function correctly to go to either "B" or "C" and then to "D" from either B or C. Both directional processes can function correctly, but only one must be correct to assure a successful outcome.

These two configurations are the most common; two others are more complex and require a more intense evaluation of the reliability system.

Series-parallel configuration is a form of both series and parallel path. It has a complexity of redundancies in which the components are in parallel and the paths are in series; the series depend on one event before the next can occur. In this configuration any failure within the structure will cause the product to be inoperative. Because it is more complex it requires a more detailed evaluation of the reliability of each component within the function of the product.

In *parallel-series configuration,* where components are in series and paths are in parallel, the first step is to obtain path reliability by statistically analyzing the product. Because of the probability of each component's effect to the reliability system, probability of failure exists. If this event occurs then the reliability system is equal to one minus the probability of a failure.

In order to apply the reliability system approach to assuring a safer product, it is important to have a sound knowledge of statistics and the concepts of reliability engineering. The essence of this chapter is to acknowledge that the reliability systems approach is valuable in building a safer product and reducing the possibility of product failure that could cause harm or peril to the end user. It can minimize the likelihood of product recall and product lawsuit by incorporating a reliability system in the design stage and by assessing the effectiveness of the product's reliability by conducting life and simulated testing.

8

Inspection and Testing Parameters

The product safety system is a preventive initiative that is integrated throughout the infrastructure of the organization; it is designed to assure that product safety is addressed and validated at each stage and discipline of the manufacturing and distribution process. Inspection and testing are two essential activities. Both of these disciplines involve the evaluation of a characteristic as it relates to a specific requirement. The requirement can be in the form of a standard, a drawing, a written instruction, a visual aid, or any other means of conveying the characteristic specification.

Inspection and testing functions can be conducted as a verification of compliance to some kind of requirement activity of a product/service item or as part of a systemic procedure. The basic premise is to determine between good and bad.

Inspection and testing evaluation can be done using the human senses (such as smell, taste, hearing, sight, and touch). Testing can be designed to assess a characteristic by attribute methods such as "go and no-go" or by how the product looks, smells, tastes, feels, and sounds. The attribute method does not measure the product; it only determines its suitability by the human sense criteria.

Inspection and testing evaluation that is made by measuring a characteristic is called "variable inspection"; it assesses the characteristic by using an instrument that actually measures the specified dimension. This evaluation is based on actual value readout. The measuring device can be an instrument such as a basic micrometer, a dial caliper, a laser, a chemical analysis, or any other precise method of gauging.

The primary purpose of inspection and testing is to assess whether products or services conform to specifications. This function is and will always be a fundamental way to determine compliance to a quality requirement and to make a disposition of the acceptance criteria. (This is often called acceptance inspection and testing.)

One of the key components of a sound inspection and testing function is the assurance of the measuring devices and/or assessment methodologies. There is an old adage by the author that states, "The measuring device is only as good as its accuracy; if the device is inaccurate, we can reject good parts, or accept bad parts. Both can be costly to the organization." From the standpoint of making a safe product, this activity is one of the most important functions.

Measuring devices and visual aids will deteriorate in accuracy during use and sometimes even in storage. For example, a nickel chrome part used as a visual aid to accept or reject a part used in a final product can become oxidized in the metal finishing environment. A metal finisher who uses this visual aid as an inspection device could begin to accept bad parts. This deterioration of a visual aid device could cost the company a great deal of money.

It is also essential that all masters used to calibrate working measuring devices be calibrated by a qualified calibration laboratory that is traceable in the United States to the National Institute of Standards and Technologies (NIST). All other industrialized countries have their own applicable calibration standard institutes.

To maintain accuracy requires a continual measuring device program consisting of nine steps:

1. Identifying all measuring devices

2. Planning a time-to-time or usage cycle for each device

3. Developing a record keeping system with an automatic method of recall

4. Providing a calibration room that is temperature and humidity controlled

5. Assuring that all master gages are calibrated to NIST on a time interval

6. Verifying that calibration checkers are qualified to check and repair devices

7. Checking all measuring devices that are on the calibration list and disposition

8. Recording all values and any rectification of each device

9. Placing measuring devices back in service or scrap devices out of the system

From a position of product safety design it is desirable to have the product safety team incorporate, as an agenda item for new and modified designs, a new test equipment and new measuring device feasibility study. The task of this agenda item would also be to review any mistake-proofing (error-proofing) devices. The team should also review test material devices and special characteristic (house-made) tooling and gauging.

Pre-production appraisal is a qualification assessment designed to judge the service capability of the product and the possible extreme applications of the product. This appraisal is also referred to as qualification inspection and testing and is akin to something called layout inspection and functional testing. This type of appraisal was designed to ensure that all customer engineering material and performance standards have been assessed prior to production.

The terms "inspector" and "tester" are holistic terms used in many types of businesses—from the building trades, safety, environmental, restaurant management, hotel management, and healthcare to the manufacturing sector. In non-manufactured goods or services, the inspection and test work is identified pertaining to a particular function (for example, building inspector, safety inspector, environmental inspector, health inspector, and so on). Today service organizations have developed greatly improved inspection and testing parameters using methods such as check-list assessments, customer follow-up surveys, and independent evaluations. These appraisal methods are designed to ensure that all specified requirements are met and to evaluate and measure non-conformities found in the system.

The initial appraisal activity in the manufacturing arena occurs during receiving or incoming material inspection and testing. The receiving appraisal is designed to assure the incoming product is not used or processed until it has been inspected or tested and found to be conforming to specific requirements.

There are many types of inspection and testing. Some of these sub-classifications have been modified to be conjoined with another function rather than to exist as a stand-alone entity. For example, many organizations have elected to eliminate incoming material inspection and testing altogether and to place this responsibility on the suppliers. Some manufacturers have chosen to verify the conformity of purchase items by applying "skip lot" inspection and testing to every lot received, providing a history of acceptable incoming inspection or testing has been established. Essentially, this skip lot inspection and testing approach means that instead of appraising every lot received, the company will inspect lots according to some random number selection routine. The skip lot appraisal will continue until a problem occurs in production or beyond, or the appraisal of the lot being inspected or tested indicates a noncompliance. If noncompliance is discovered, the organization will go back to appraising every lot received.

Another type of appraisal is the in-process inspection and testing function. Many companies have merged this function into the manufacturing operation; the operator is responsible for characteristic compliance and is judged by production output as well as compliance to quality requirements. Although appraisal results should be recorded and maintained as a record of disposition, there is a caveat. Operators should not simply accept a bad setup or fail to identify noncompliant parts produced on their machines. This situation occurs when the manufacturing supervisor is more motivated by quantity of production output than by quality of product. This objective is often passed down to the operator.

If the in-process appraisal is judged to be ineffective for any reason, then "final inspection and testing" is designed to ensure that finished components and product are not dispatched until all activities have been satisfactorily completed and there is a verification of the in-process quality assurance. This function should be conducted solely by the quality assurance department and recorded for proper disposition of product.

Although many manufacturers have a manual appraisal function at final inspection and testing and it functions quite successfully with a high degree of reliability and assurance, many organizations have elected to automate the final appraisal. For example, golf balls and eggs are 100% tested for oversize and undersize characteristics; the acceptable item is passed on and the unacceptable item is side-railed for disposition.

There are gages today that automatically check 100% for concentricity, eccentricity, and ovality conformance. It is not uncommon for manufacturers to move toward total automation or semi-automated appraisal by production processes. Within this movement of evaluation acceptance, the appraisal function becomes integrated into the operational function and verified by dock (audit) inspection and testing before the product is shipped.

Dock auditing is designed to assure that the product and its ancillary functions (such as packaging, identification, warranty materials, and so on) are released to the customer conforming to all quality requirements. In augmentation to dock auditing is "shipping inspection and testing," which is designed to assure that all shipped products conform to requirements.

Organizations that do not have an in-process operation will rely on a final appraisal and a detailed production part approval process (PPAP) for conformance decisions. PPAP and initial sample inspection and test (ISIT) are critical assessment tools for new and modified products. They are designed to assure customers that the first production run will be in conformance with all designated characteristics and that the company will retain the actual characteristic measurements and attribute evaluations data on file, and if applicable, submit actual characteristic measurements and attribute evaluations to the customer.

An ancillary appraisal function that is internal to the organization's processes is called "process systems auditing." This appraisal function is designed to ensure compliance with all documents derived from policies, procedures, and instructions of the overall organizational system, to correct any non-conformities found in the system, and to verify that corrective action was effective.

These appraisal types are primarily designed to assure that product is designed and manufactured to conform to the organization's quality assurance system, all governmental regulations, and the customer's requirements. Some organizations may need to build an appraisal system around all of the sub-classifications:

1. Incoming material and component inspection and testing
2. In-process inspection and testing
3. Final inspection and testing
4. Pre-production inspection and testing
5. Dock inspection
6. Service inspection and testing
7. Initial sample inspection and testing
8. Production part approval process inspection and testing
9. Shipping inspection and testing
10. Process shipping

Inspector, testers, and auditors should be trained to understand the component, the products, the standards, the instruments, the equipment, and the processes. Once trained and qualified, they are given the job of making the appraisal and of judging its conformance. This is the time to determine whether the component or product is fit for use. If the component or product is conforming to the requirements, it is identified as good, recorded as such, and passed on to finished goods, packaging, and shipping. But if the component or product is nonconforming, rework or added operations may bring it back into conformance. It is then re-inspected or tested and recorded; if found to be in conformance, it is packaged and shipped.

Two other dispositions can occur: "scrap" the component or product or "use as is."

If the decision is to scrap the component or product, the part or container is identified as scrap and it is forwarded to a scrap bin or scrap area before being physically removed from the facility. This activity is recorded and the data retained (in some cases it is required to physically destroy the part).

The other disposition for a nonconforming component or product is to "use as is." This should be done only with the consent of the customer if it is a customer design. However, if the component or product is a manufacturer's proprietary design or a commercial item, the disposition requires the proper sign-off of the organization's management personnel. Typically a representative from design engineering and quality assurance and a representative from executive management are required for disposition.

These three individuals should apply this option only as a last resort and every attempt should be made to correct future design and manufacturing issues that might have caused this condition. All records of this disposition should be retained for the life of the product or an acceptable time.

The dispositions should be analyzed for trend analysis and for the effectiveness of all corrective action of non-conformities. These activities should be recorded and retained. The lack of good record keeping can jeopardize the company's position in a court action. The organization should allow sufficient time to investigate nonconformity, to assure that the best possible solution has occurred, and to assure that records of this action are readily available.

The following is a guide to disposition action:

- Accept item – record and retain data and move item forward

- Reject item and scrap – record and retain data and obtain corrective action (C/A), verify C/A effectiveness, and remove scrapped item from process

- Reject item and rework – record and retain data and obtain C/A, verify C/A effectiveness, and rework item to a plan to bring back into conformity, then re-inspect and disposition

- Reject item and execute extra operations – record and retain data and obtain C/A, verify C/A effectiveness, conduct extra operation to a plan to bring back into conformity, then re-inspect and disposition

- Reject item and "use as is" – record and retain data and obtain C/A, verify C/A effectiveness, and move item forward

The proper disposition of items and the investigation of all non-conformities is a critical element of the quality assurance function and should never be taken lightly.

The prime purpose of the appraisal function is to assure that manufacturing processes (from procurement to shipping) meet the requirements set forth by product design. But without an effective inspection and test plan, the appraisal function will lack continuity between the design parameters and the manufacturing processes. The plan is the bridge between the two.

For each appraisal location an inspection and test plan should be developed by a quality engineer or quality leader (the planner) to be used by the inspector or tester to appraise the product. This plan should include quality characteristics to be checked as determined by input from:

- The product and process specifications

- The customer's requirements

- Applicable industry standards and other general-use sources
- Third-party requirements
- Customer expectations
- Governmental and regulatory requirements

Aligned with the appraisal function is the ancillary equipment used for testing at strategic stages of the fabrication and any standard and special gauges used for characteristic compliance. Information incorporated into the plan includes the semantics of wording, the classification of characteristics for seriousness, sample schemes used for product appraisal, and any visual aids, product samples, and photographs.

The plan is used for the set-up of automated inspection and testing equipment and integrated process appraisal. Where there is no tangible product that requires an assessment of dimension, appearance, or testing parameters, the main source of evaluation is the checklist. The checklist appraisal plan can be developed as a standard of that particular industry (hotels, financial institutions, restaurants, healthcare), or the plan may be constructed by a member of the management team.

Under the umbrella of product safety is the "seriousness classification."

The first level of composite definitions is the "minor defect." This defect will not cause injury or harm to the end-user, it will not affect usability of the product, and it is unlikely to be noticed by the customer. It may affect appearance but it conforms completely to regulations and has no impact on product safety.

The second level is the "major B defect." This defect will not cause injury or harm to the end user, but it will make the product more difficult to use and it will be an annoyance if noticed by the user. It may require product replacement but not in the category of a recall.

The third level is the "major A defect." This defect may render the product unfit for use, may cause rejection by the end-user, and will likely reduce product marketability. It may cause the organization to lose customers and may result in losses greater than the value of the product; it will fail to conform to regulations.

The fourth level is the "critical defect." This defect will cause personal injury or harm to the end-user and will render the product totally unfit for use. Essentially, the organization will be exposed to a product recall and subject to product liability litigation.

The inspection and testing functions should be designed to assure that critical and major A classifications are addressed and every effort should be made to incorporate "error proofing" wherever possible.

9

Operational Efficiencies

The word *operation* has a broad connotation. In the context of this subject an operation is a process developed around an existing infrastructure or the modification of a process to incorporate features that will enhance and/or provide for a safe, reliable, and durable product. Operational efficiencies include how the product is made in the most efficient manner using mistake proofing, automatic evaluations, and other appraisal tools to assure that each operation is conducted correctly. It will also include "process mapping" for efficient flow of materials and sub-assemblies, and describe how the processes can be improved to consistently meet or exceed quality requirements.

Process mapping is a holistic activity that starts at the "fuzzy front end" of the product inception stage and concludes at the expiration of the product at the post-production stage. Between these two events the product is exposed to a series of operations. The initial operation is the design stage. It can be broken down into sub-operations. Each operation should have a system of review and be signed-off by an unbiased team of knowledgeable assignees. For example, the design operation should have a design review activity and a product safety activity among its functions. These operations should have a description of their activities, and that function should itself be reviewed for accuracy and correctness.

The expiration of the product can be identified as a single operation. How did it expire? It might have become obsolete and replaced by a new generation of product. This has been common in the manufacturing of cell phones, computers, televisions, and other high-tech items. In this case the product was not defective, misused, or abused; it did, in fact, meet its intended application without flaw, only to be replaced by an improved product.

Some items are designed to expire within a specific time or usage period, and that can be evaluated as to empirical life cycle data. For example, a typical light bulb is designed to function for an average of 750 hours before it fails. If it obtains a minus three standard deviation (least amount of time allowed by the manufacturer), it is deemed to have met the life cycle requirements. This operation would require actual data from the field, or more practical, a simulated life cycle test in the company's reliability lab. This operational method is common in many products, and this data should be logged and evaluated for its efficiencies and signed off as performed correctly and reviewed.

The most disconcerting answer is a field failure that was caused by either the customer's misuse or abuse of the product or a foreseeable or unforeseeable weakness in the design or manufacturing operation that subsequently caused harm or injury to the user of that product. This sub-operation evaluation requires a detailed investigation as to the reason for the failure and requires documentation of the resolve. This is a critical operation that necessitates a final review and sign-off verifying that the operation was conducted and recorded and that it was validated as an effective and efficient solution.

POST-PRODUCTION ACTIVITIES

Up to this point we have discussed how operational efficiencies are critical to the internal processes of the organization, and how to handle failures in the field. The key to the effectiveness of a good operational system is the efficiencies in which it exists. This same initiative can apply to products that require maintenance in the usage environment. In this situation the product has changed ownership from the manufacturer to the customer. Even though the product operations have been transferred, the manufacturer still is subject to product liability even if the product has been misused or abused.

The manufacturer, therefore, has a responsibility to assure that a maintenance instruction accompanies the product to the field. This instruction should provide that the individual who is actually performing the maintenance would not be injured. The procedure and instruction communiqué must be written to be user friendly and must address all safety concerns. Improper maintenance, anything that could possibly result in injury or damage to the maintenance technician or user of the product, must be reviewed by the manufacturer and be subject to a corrective actions of the procedures and / or instructions.

Another maintenance concern is failure to perform maintenance on time or at all. Failure to properly maintain a systematic maintenance program may cause the part to wear out and fail, resulting in an accident or at least causing the product not to function. Each potential failure resulting from improper maintenance must be reviewed and evaluated to determine whether harm or injury may occur.

The maintenance function requires a personnel skill level suitable to the type of product requiring maintenance. If personnel are not properly trained, the possibility of a tool or other object being left in the product or an erroneous procedure being performed is highly likely. The designer must provide safeguards and a validation checklist.

The lack of a maintenance program or an ineffective maintenance program could result in damage to other components. For example, a semi-truck engine failed after several months of traveling dirt roads. The main cause was failure of the technician to change oil regularly, coupled with the truck owner's failure to provide a maintenance program for the air filter. In this situation the maintenance program was weak and the exposure to failure was quite high.

An engine that becomes inoperative and causes a truck to fail is serious and can cause an injury in certain circumstances, but this maintenance safety issue pales in comparison with the possibility that a school bus engine would fail due to an ineffective and non-efficient maintenance program. A failure of a school bus on a mountain in Colorado because of an inoperative engine could result in peril to the children on the bus. Needless to say the magnitude of this failure requires serious attention to resolve.

When designing a product it's important to consider that it might be maintained by professionals or by people who do their own maintenance to save on cost. In order to reduce or eliminate improper maintenance methods or simply the lack of a maintenance initiative, the organization must have in place a sound post-production procedure; if applicable, it's important to supply supporting instructions on why and how to execute an effective and efficient maintenance program.

The most effective way to minimize poor maintenance practices might be to consider how the product could be designed without features that require post-production maintenance activities. For example, designing a gas furnace with a greaseless bearing would eliminate the need for the furnace motor to be oiled at specified intervals. Likewise, designing an automatic greenhouse sprinkler system with a time setting would eliminate a maintenance function. Today all vehicles are designed without spark plugs or separate alternators; automobile owners no longer perform routine maintenance or have it done by an automotive technician.

It is important that the manufacturer design and produce a product that is "user friendly," and that the maintenance and field repair activities are simplified as much as possible. Also important is the integration of safety features in the design and production stages. Several years ago manufacturers felt that their responsibility ended once the product was in the customer's hands, and that the express warranty period was a terminus. However, the courts held that the manufacturer's liability does not end there, but only at the end of the product life. Thus, all safety issues must be addressed and resolved throughout the duration of the product's life cycle, and these issues must be recorded and verified for effectiveness. This includes operational maintenance problems as well.

Manufacturers must also initiate a proactive plan for problems that could arise because of the need for product maintenance and repair. One effective method of accomplishing this activity is to develop a checklist of maintenance plan criteria. The checklist should address concerns such as these:

- Could the maintenance operation or repair cause harm or peril to the person performing the work?

- Are procedures and instructions available to the person performing the work?

- Are procedures and instructions clear and understandable?

- Do procedures and instructions indicate when protected equipment must be used because a hazard might exist?

This short list of potential problems is only an example of what kinds of questions a manufacturer may want to incorporate into their plan. It's important to recognize that a manufacturer's failure to develop a post-production maintenance and repair initiative could result in a product liability lawsuit.

Manufacturers should design product with the least complexity possible so as to minimize maintenance problems. They should use "error proofing" and "mistake proofing" whenever possible…and other fail-safe designs to prevent harm or peril to the user. They should design the product to provide for easy access to the maintenance area for effortless checking, service, and replacement of product components. They should develop procedures that will minimize the possibility of maintenance problems. And they should design the product to minimize the possibility of injury to the maintenance person while performing the task.

10

Product Safety in the Service Sector

Most people envision product safety as an activity pertaining only to manufacturing and most lawsuits focus on tangible products such as automobiles, lawn tractors, electric saws, and so forth. However, many products are classified under the *service* umbrella and those products are also affected by safety issues. In this context, *service* is defined as "an act of giving assistance or advantage to another or anything useful, with a value to benefit the user."

This chapter will address several types of service sectors and will illustrate a paradigm for developing a safe product that can be used in all service-related industries. The basic concept is designed around a question format with follow-up procedures and instructions and a "check sheet" process.

Virtually every service is designed to provide a benefit to the user. Some services are more complex than others and are made up of several sub-functions. For example, a sub-function for a cruise ship line is the food service department. The food service department has to plan breakfast, lunch, and dinner menus as well as provide ancillary foods, snacks, and drinks for its passengers. This food must be prepared on time, served at the proper temperature, and taste good. If the food is mishandled, improperly stored, or purchased without a receiving inspection it could harm the passengers. A bad batch of meats, eggs, or any other food could cause sickness within the ship's confines and result in an unfavorable reaction among the cruise guests and perhaps a lawsuit.

Salmonella, botulism, and other bacteria raise their ugly heads when the director of food services fails to have or fails to follow a prescribed process to assure proper food handling and storage. Does the ship's quality system have a specific procedure and subsequent instructions for proper food control? If yes, is this system being evaluated for compliance from time to time?

Each of the ship's sub-functions is subject to failures that could cause harm or injury to the passenger of the ship. Another example of the ship's operation is the entertainment activity. This function is designed to keep guests actively involved in entertaining events, but some events can be harmful to participants if not properly executed and supervised.

For example, after a night of gambling or dancing, with plenty of drinking going on, a guest decides to go for a midnight swim and drowns. The entertainment director had previously elected not to have a lifeguard on duty after 11:00 p.m. and instead put a sign by the pool stating "No lifeguard on duty after 11:00 p.m." Although this is a clear and noticeable express warning, does it nullify the ship's responsibility? If the drowned person's family decides to sue the cruise ship line, the court may focus on the possibility that a guest, intoxicated or not, may simply ignore the sign and swim anyway. The plaintiff's attorney most likely would claim that ship management should have anticipated the foreseeable possibility that an accident like this might occur and should have taken steps to prevent it.

The ship's management could have taken one or more courses of preventive actions. It could have encircled the pool area with a fence of sufficient height and a gate that could be locked after 11:00 p.m. Or it could have made a lifeguard available upon request during the off hours.

The cruise ship has many sub-functions that should be examined in order to prevent or minimize harm to its guests. One effective way to do this assessment is to contract with an outside consulting firm to form a service safety team, select participants, and facilitate the team's efforts. Using such techniques as brainstorming, knowledge mapping, the morphological box, and problem reformulation will aid in the safety identification process. These tools are but examples of the many techniques an organization can use in order to evaluate conditions that might cause harm to the user of the services.

The service safety team should develop a checklist of criteria that can be used to appraise compliance to specific rules, procedures, and instructions that were developed from the team's activities. Any deficiencies found from the appraisal audit must be reviewed and a corrective action immediately implemented to resolve the situation. This evaluation should be conducted at specified intervals and all the findings documented for future analysis. The analysis should assess overall performance of the service as it relates to good customer satisfaction and determine any trends that might indicate problems or positive forecast of future customer relations.

The safety team should also develop a method to determine the pulse of the customer by using tools such as surveys, interviews, and other modes of customer communication. This evaluation will aid the organization in identifying problems or potential problems with the service they provide and assessing whether these problems involve the safety of the customer.

The manufacturing sector is easy to identify. Essentially, it encompasses any organization that makes a tangible product. In the service sector there are no limits to product type (service). Restaurant, hotel and motel management, grocery stores, movie theaters, healthcare organizations, educational facilities, and department stores are examples of the service industry.

Any service organization is subject to an internal review of product safety potentials. Without a formal review and documented evidence of that review, the service organization can be exposed to a lawsuit for harm or injury to the customer.

One of the most common lawsuits against grocery stores is the "slip and fall" scam. A person will spill water on an aisle floor and then pretend to fall because the floor is slippery. In this situation there was no intent or failure on the part of the store to expose the customer to injury, but the problem of perceived injury did occur. What can the store do? One suggestion is to place video cameras in each aisle to detect such incidents.

However, sometimes liquids are spilled and there may be other reasons for the floor to be slippery. Stores should have a safety team to correct or minimize situations like this. For example, many stores purchase a special floor mat for areas that could become slippery.

Restaurant management is one of the most vulnerable service categories due to the multi-complexity of its service. From the time the customer enters the parking lot to the time he or she leaves, the potential for harm or injury exists. Ice in the parking lot or on the sidewalk, spoiled food, excessively hot liquids, foreign matter in the food—all are conditions that might cause harm or injury to the customer. The restaurant owner or manager should solicit a product safety expert or at least form an internal team to review the potential accidents and take the necessary steps to correct or improve the existing system.

Sometimes product users cause harm or injury by the misapplication of a product. A misused chain saw, a mishandled lawn mower, or the injection of the wrong dose of a medication are examples of how someone can cause an accident. Sometimes accidents are simply accidents. Someone entering a building may trip over his own feet, fall, and break an arm; someone in a bowling facility may drop a bowling ball on her foot. These mishaps are clearly the responsibility of the user. No matter how hard the manufacturer or the service organization attempts to prevent accidents, it is impossible to predict every mishap. Sometimes the best safety initiative will not be good enough to prevent harm.

Hotel and motel management is a complex, multi-service industry. Like the healthcare industry and the cruise ship business, it is made up of many sub-processes. The main component is sleeping comfort for hotel guests, along with exercise equipment and swimming facilities. Another component is the restaurant function. Not all hotels or motels have restaurants, but the ones that offer food service must address the concerns and issues of a stand-alone restaurant.

Each one of these sub-functions must be reviewed for safety issues and all concerns addressed. After the consultant and/or safety team has identified areas of concern and taken steps to improve them, it should develop a checklist. This checklist is used to convert the statement made concerning the safety issue into a question. For example, guests should not have to stand in line more than ten minutes check in and check out. The question would be "how long does the guest wait in line?" Many senior citizens find it difficult to stand for a period of time and this condition does have an impact on the health and the safety of the guest. The safety auditor will want to observe, with an unbiased sample, the time it actually takes to process the guest at registration. These evaluations should be conducted at peak times (mid to late afternoon and early morning).

In addition to recording actual data, the safety audit should include a column for compliance acceptance and one for non-compliance. This checklist can be designed using the Likert method illustrated here:

Full compliance = 3

Partial compliance = 2

Marginal compliance = 1

Non-compliance = 0

Using the Likert method, the checklist designer can easily quantify the audit by a numerical score and establish a baseline for compliance and improvement criteria. The checklist should be constructed to evaluate safety issues and to document corrective actions taken. It is good practice to design the checklist in sub-categories to match the sub-functions of the organization. This action would allow for the evaluation of each sub-function's performance separate from other activities.

The checklist evaluation and the customer survey are the two main tools the service sector can use to identify potential safety issues, but there are other ways to determine whether service activity may cause harm or injury. For example, an orderly in a hospital notices that the main entrance light has burned out. This condition may cause someone to fall. A waiter in a restaurant notices that a wooden chair is cracked. This could cause the chair to collapse under the weight of the next person who sits down.

Many situations that could result in harm or injury to the customer in the service sector may not be depicted by a checklist audit or survey. Every organization, regardless of service provided, should encourage all employees to be aware of potentially harmful situations and report problems immediately to a supervisor. Good practice calls for the installation of a safety observation system (SOS). This system uses an observation form designed to describe the concern and the observer's judgment of the magnitude of the SOS (for example, urgent concern, major concern, or marginally unsafe).

A product safety initiative is just as important in the service sector as it is in the manufacturing sector. To address only the hardware aspect of product safety is to fail to be the watchdog of overall product safety. Regardless of the service provided or the method used to detect safety concerns, the organization should consider the possibility of abuse or misuse of that service. In this context *abuse* means "to treat it so badly that you damage it." *Misuse* means "to use it wrongly." In healthcare, for example, the abuse factor may involve an arm sling the doctor has installed to protect a patient's broken arm. The patient may elect to take it off, causing damage to his arm. The misuse factor might involve taking twice as much medication as the doctor prescribed, causing the user harm.

Another example of abuse occurs in the service sector in the hotel business. A customer is sitting at a table by the swimming pool. After a few beers he slams his drink hard on the table and breaks the glass. A piece of the glass cuts a bystander and the bystander sues the hotel for allowing alcohol and glass containers in the pool area while people are only partially dressed.

Using the hotel swimming pool example again we can discuss a safety issue as it applies to misuse. The pool is protected from outsiders by a fence with a locked gate. The pool is officially closed at 10:00 p.m., but a guest who attempts to climb over the fence falls and is injured and then sues the hotel claiming an unsafe condition. This event seems ridiculous and certainly unfair to the hotel owner, who made a concerted effort to prevent injury to anyone around the pool site. Yet in a lawsuit there are no limits and often suits have no legitimacy.

The only thing an organization can do is to develop a sound safety plan, incorporate an effective "product/service safety audit" to validate the plan, and minimize the possibility of a lawsuit. There are other steps a hotel and other organizations can take to strengthen their safety initiatives.

One hotel with an excellent reputation for quality and safety has developed a written quality and safety system that clearly reduces their exposure to a lawsuit. The general manager has made a commitment to providing a safe environment for his guests and has installed cameras to monitor all the floor hallways, the swimming pool, the exercise room, the elevators, and all around the outside of the building. Except for the main lobby, all doors are locked and require key entry. The swimming pool is enclosed with a high fence that is almost impossible to climb, the outside gates to the pool area are locked after a specific time, and the only way to the pool is from within the complex. Other features of the pool area include Styrofoam, rather than air-filled, life preservers and several life-hooks. At high check-in times there are enough reservation clerks at the front desk to prevent a guest from waiting too long. In the eating area there are plenty of tables and chairs; all the guests are able to sit and eat without having to wait. All emergency exits are clear of obstructions. The parking areas are well lighted and the traffic patterns are well planned to prevent congestion and potential accidents. Guest rooms are clean and the shower has an extra-large grab bar. Hotel hospitality is excellent and the restaurant manager has a great attitude for his job and the guests whom he serves. He has provided a safe environment where people are able to move around the eating area without worrying about slipping and falling. The general manager and his employees are quick to respond to any safety concerns.

This hotel is but an example of the many good hotels and other service businesses that have addressed quality and safety issues. The safety system should always be a part of the overall business plan. It is an ongoing initiative that must be audited from time to time to assure the organization's safety effectiveness. This safety system applied to virtually all types of service providers, as well as all basic manufacturing facilities, and any deficiencies found in the system must be corrected immediately.

Unfortunately, not all service providers are keen on making the environment as safe as possible and only care to "get away" with the bare necessities. For example, I recently stayed at a hotel that had booked a wedding party and my room was sandwiched between two guest rooms whose occupants partied literally all night. Knowing I had to get up early to drive to my next lecture appointment, I called down to the desk twice to let the hotel clerk know of the situation. She came to the floor twice and tried to quiet the guests, but to no avail. The guests kept me up all night. With virtually no sleep I got up at 6:00 a.m., checked out of the hotel, and drove the seven hours to my next appointment. About a quarter of the way there I momentarily dosed off at the wheel, but quickly regained consciousness and stopped at a rest area to sleep for a while.

But what if I had an accident and caused injury or death to someone or myself? Who would be at fault, me or the hotel for not providing a quiet environment for their guest? If this hypothetical accident had caused peril to someone, it is highly likely that a lawsuit would have resulted. In the final adjudication, who would have been found to be at fault, the driver or the hotel that had neglected to take a more affirmative action? Remember, the main business of a hotel is to provide customers with a safe, quiet, and comfortable place to sleep. Was this done?

Using a "cause and effect" analysis, we see that the accident was caused by the driver and the effect was the accident. But actually the cause (the driver) becomes the effect, and the real cause becomes the hotel's failure to assure that the wedding party was quiet. Drilling further into the example, we see that the real cause was hotel guests who partied all night, keeping another guest awake; the hotel was the effect.

Since the hotel was in the "main stream of commerce" and the guest contracted with the hotel directly, the guest who was subject to the noise could sue the hotel on the grounds failure to provide a safe and quiet environment for sleep. Could this be considered a frivolous lawsuit, or is this justification? Certainly this situation is open for discussion. A good defendant attorney and a good expert witness may play a key part in how the case is adjudicated.

Many lawsuits in the service sector may be perceived as unjust, but they happen consistently, with judgments settled out of court and payouts to plaintiffs worth several thousands of dollars. In order to prevent this situation it is critical that service organizations develop a product safety initiative and document all actions.

Regardless of the service provided—be it banking, wedding coordination, lawn care, entertainment concerts, or any of the previous examples—the service organization should have mechanics in place to examine whether the service has the potential for causing harm or injury to the user of the service. If that determination has been made, then immediate steps should be taken to assure that safeguards are in place to minimize or eliminate that harm or injury.

Most of what a business or individual does requires multiple services. For example, when we wake up in the morning and get ready for work we use a service that provides electricity for our air conditioner in the summer months, for our alarm clock, and for the light beside the bed. Electricity use continues throughout the day. We use water for our bath, for brushing out teeth, for our toilet usage, for our morning coffee, and so on. We use natural gas service to keep us warm in the winter months. While at work we use gas, water, and electricity for all kinds of things. In the evening when we shop, go to a bowling alley or restaurant, or simply return home we use electricity, water, and gas.

Harm or injury could result from service failures. For example, let's suppose a transformer blew on our street and that failure caused our electric service to go out for a few days while we were not home. This failure caused the meat in our refrigerator to spoil and we, not realizing it was bad, ate the meat and got sick. Is the failure due to "mother nature," meaning no one is at fault? Or is it the fault of the electric service company that failed to have a good preventive maintenance program or a backup transformer system?

Many organizations in the service industry don't realize that environmental conditions and malfunctioning service actions have the potential to cause harm or injury to customers, clients, or even employees. For example, a wholesale store with a membership fee hired four ladies to serve samples of a food product. These ladies, ranging in age from 71 to 89, were required to stand beside a sample cart for seven hours each day, three days a week. Two of the ladies appeared to be fatigued by the end of the day, and this fatigue could cause them to fall and injure themselves. Should the store provide stools for the ladies to sit on? This would seem like a quick and easy solution to prevent a potential safety problem. But would this action cause others problems for the store? Should employees in the bakery department, the meat department, and the checkout area also have stools, even though they are not in that age group? What if someone is injured falling off a stool? Would the store be responsible for not providing a stool of the right height?

The actions and decisions of an organization can unintentionally place that organization in a vulnerable position and open them up for a potential lawsuit. Thus discussions in this book apply as much to the service industry as to the manufacturing sector.

11

Product Liability
Lawsuits and Judgments

Discussions in this chapter about litigation cases and product recalls are offered to assist an organization in sidestepping the pitfalls of improper design or manufacturing process, failure to warn, and failure to follow a course of effective product safety practices. The lawsuits discussed here are the primarily result of erroneous product use or use of a product that exhibited a design or production defect.

Each case presented in this chapter involves a failure within the defendant's organization to prevent the mishap. A *mishap* is defined as an unfortunate accident. Most accidents are not intentionally orchestrated or caused by a company's lack of caring for the safety of the user. Instead, they are caused by failure to provide a product safety initiative or motivated by a drive to reduce internal cost.

Many situations cause an organization or individual to deviate from an objective and thus create a deficiency. For example, my wife and I have two homes in two different cities of the same state and keep vehicles in both residences. My wife purchased license stickers for our five vehicles in one of the cities. We placed stickers on four vehicles at the main residence, but forgot to take the remaining sticker to the second residence for that car. A few weeks later, while driving the spare car at that residence, I was stopped by a police officer who told me that I was driving without displaying a license sticker. He recommended that I put the sticker on my license plate as soon as possible.

This happening was initiated by the need to procure five license stickers so that my wife and I can meet the state vehicle code for another year. The process, something all car and truck owners do on an annual basis, was successfully done for four of the five vehicles. Failure to bring a sticker for the car at the second residence caused this nonconformity.

This particular situation did not cause harm or peril to anyone and did not have an adverse effect on anything, but it was still a deficiency to a requirement and a candidate for action to prevent a future occurrence.

Many such cases will not result in a negative risk, hazard, or harm to anyone, but still reflect a flaw in a process.

A lawsuit did not result from the previous example, but most lawsuits are the result of a flaw in a product or service design, a manufacturing process, a failure to warn, or a failure to meet a systemic objective. Sometimes a product recall can minimize or even prevent a lawsuit, but recalls are costly to the manufacturer and damage the organization's image in the marketplace. The alternative is lawsuits and/or regulatory fines.

The legal profession is a prime driver and main motivator behind lawsuits initiated against an organization that exhibits a "deep pocket" sales base. Essentially any company with sales of $100 million or more is a candidate for a potential legal action. For example, in the case of *Bell v. Alltel Communications, LLC,* case no.: 2:08-CV-00648, a class action lawsuit resulted in a court judgment against Alltel. This settlement resolves a lawsuit over whether Alltel violated certain requirements imposed by the Fair and Accurate Credit Transaction Act (FACTA).

Alltel denied liability, but agreed to a proposed settlement to all persons who received an electronically printed receipt from Alltel in a credit card or debit card transaction occurring at an Alltel retail store location within a specific time frame, or in a credit card or debit card transaction involving the purchase of Alltel's "Phone in a Box" products within a specific time period.

The settlement states that all people who are eligible may receive a voucher for up to $5.00 toward the purchase of a wireless telephone accessory (excluding cell phones) or 100 minutes of free long distance service. The settlement entitles people who engaged in a credit card or debit card transaction as described above to compensation and releases Alltel from any liability. Note: This class action lawsuit agreement was predicated on the court's approval of the settlement.

Many of the eligible people will not pursue a $5.00 voucher with limitations. But what is interesting is that the court-appointed lawyers for the class action will ask the court for attorney's fees and costs, in the aggregate amount of $180,000, to be paid separately by Alltel. This is a good example of why the legal profession is motivated to take on a lawsuit regardless of whether it has legitimacy or whether the plaintiffs will receive a reasonable compensation. And because most lawsuits are taken on a contingency basis, the attorney's fees and costs are paid by the defendant...particularly if the defendant has "deep pockets."

But regardless of whether the lawsuit has justification, the defendant (manufacturer or service type) must be prepared for an arduous, costly, and sometimes prolonged litigation process. In the aforementioned case neither the plaintiff nor any class member had sustained actual personal harm or even monetary injury as a result of the issues in this litigation. However, the FACTA law requires that the expiration date be deleted from credit and debit card receipts presented to customers at the point of sale.

WHAT IS A CLASS ACTION?

In a class action, one or more people sue a defendant to receive compensation as settlement for an alleged wrong. In the previous example, Elizabeth R. Bell sued on behalf of people who had similar claims. All these people are identified as class members and the plaintiff's attorney is referred to as class council. In a class action only one court resolves the issues for all class members, except for those who exclude themselves from the class action.

In a settlement the court does not decide in favor of either side, and both plaintiff and defendant think they could have prevailed at trial. In most class action suits there is no trial and both sides agree to a settlement. In this manner both avoid the cost of a trial and the people affected receive compensation. In most cases the defendant pays the plaintiffs a specific amount of money or other tangible assets and usually pays both parties' legal costs.

WHAT IS PRODUCT LIABILITY AND DOES IT COST THE DEFENDANT?

Product liability is the legal definition used to describe an event whereby an injury or financial loss results in individuals or a business seeking compensation. In the product liability litigation process the plaintiff seeks to be compensated for injury allegedly caused by a defective product manufactured by the defendant. The plaintiff's attorney must prove that the defective product caused the client to suffer injury or financial loss due to the inadequate performance of the product or negligence of the defendant.

Toyota's reputation for quality and reliability was tarnished after the Japanese automaker recalled more than ten million cars for sudden acceleration problems and other injurious conditions. These problems forced the automaker to go public with "damage control" to overcome the overwhelming negative reaction by American car owners. The company faced hundreds of lawsuits alleging that some models could speed up out of the driver's control, potentially resulting in crash injuries and deaths. Initially Toyota went on the defense and claimed that drivers were at fault. They also blamed faulty floor mats and sticky pedals for the acceleration problem.

The Toyota story is an excellent example of how one product defect event can destroy and negate the accomplishments and destroy the reputation of an organization that was previously a leader in the marketplace. The year after the product defect recall the company's United States sales dropped to an all time low, exhibiting just 0.2% rise while the rest of the industry's overall sales climbed more than 11% for that year.

Toyota was not the only automaker exposed to a product liability problem that year. At about the same time Ford had a major recall. Sean Bowman was driving a classmate to a community college when the rear axle of his Ford Windstar cracked in half, sending the minivan careening out of control and into a building and killing him. His family said a safety recall notice from Ford was received in the mail the following week. The notice stated that the 2001 Windstar's axle should be checked as soon as possible because it could corrode and break.

Bowman's family and some safety experts are questioning why Ford failed to give the recall the urgency it deserved. Even after Ford recognized the product defect, they procrastinated and failed to let Bowman know of the defect until more than six weeks after they initially announced the recall. Even after the recall Ford appeared to have ancillary problems (unavailable repair parts and extended scheduling delays). Windstar owners had to wait several months.

Ford's product defect problem affected approximately 575,000 older Windstar models (1998 to 2003) recalled in the United States and Canada. According to the National Highway Traffic Safety Administration, auto makers are required by federal law to notify owners by mail within a reasonable time; owners are typically notified within 30 days.

Toyota and Ford are examples of the many product liability cases and recalls that occur in the automobile industry. Automobiles are complex products with many sub-components and virtually all auto makers have been affected by product safety issues. Flaws in design or manufacturing processes, coupled with unforeseeable use of the vehicle, can result in product safety issues. In the final analysis, it is the responsibility of the manufacturer or distributor to assure that products are safe and reliable.

Even a product that is not officially classified as defective can appear to be harmful to the user. An example is the Schlitz Brewery Company. Schlitz was the largest beer manufacturer in the world in the 1950s and held that position for more than ten years…no brewery was even close. But because the company's chief executive had mandated the company show a bigger profit margin, the manufacturing department reduced the time of fermentation. This change in process, without proper research and qualification, caused an enzyme to develop. White particles began to appear in the bottles after a short time on store shelves.

In 1976, the Schlitz Brewery Company had to destroy several million bottles of beer. This played a major role in the company's fall from its position as world leader. It was eventually bought out. This lack of direction and "silo" building from within the organization, along with in-fighting, caused the company to lose control of established and proven processes, both in manufacturing and organizational structure.

This example did not highlight a product defect that subsequently resulted in a lawsuit, but it did illustrate a condition that appeared to be a defect in the eyes of the purchaser. Here is the caveat: A change in manufacturing processes can adversely affect customer perception of an organization, and may result in a lawsuit based on a negative visional and taste deviation from what the consumer normally expects. In the Schlitz example the enzyme change did not cause physiological harm to the consumer, but it did create a psychological perception that there might be harm.

Recently General Motors had a situation, similar to Ford's rear axle problem, that resulted in a recall of more than 25,000 cars. General Electric faced a recall involving a defective toaster with an electrical malfunction that could result in the toaster catching fire. Many thousands of toasters were recalled.

Many lawsuits are not the result of just manufacturer, design, or intrinsic defects. This next court case cited by Mr. Randall Goodden, a key speaker at the ASQ 2011 Annual Product Safety & Liability Prevention Conference in Milwaukee, Wisconsin, is an excellent example of how a non-product defect can contribute to the harm of the end user. In 2010 Natalie M. Barnhard, a physical therapy assistant, was rendered a quadriplegic while working out at Amherst Orthopedic Physical Therapy in Buffalo, New York. A 600-pound Cybec Classic leg extension weight machine fell on her, crushing her vertebrae, when she leaned on the machine to stretch her shoulder. It took four people to pull the machine off of Barnhard.

The New York jury came back with a $66,000,000 verdict against Cybec. Cybec International, a company with annual sales of $117,000,000, had only $4,000,000 worth of product liability insurance. This company had an excellent reputation for fine and safe exercise machines and a history of designing a solidly built product. However, misuse of a product for something other than what was intended can expose any organization to a lawsuit and virtually run that company out of business. Although the Cybec design included bolt holes for securing the machine to the floor, it is the responsibility of the installer to properly secure the machine. Even after this terrible accident it's possible to find exercise machines that are not secured to the floor. They could put a person misusing the machine in harm's way and expose the manufacturer to product liability litigation.

Countless lawsuits and recalls have been generated over the last several decades in the United States alone. Many are frivolous, but many have merit. Regardless of whether the case has merit, the litigation and recall costs can be extremely expensive, and the organization's image is at stake.

12
Types of Product Failure

The types of product failure are many in the manufacturing industry and in the service sector. We can categorize these failures into six classifications. Each organization's product safety review team should identify their potentials for failures and then, using creativity tools, place these failures into these classifications.

What does it mean to be creative in product safety and product liability prevention?

Creativity involves the ability of the team to brainstorm potential failure and make an unbiased evaluation between the failure type and unrelated happenings, facts, observations, conditions, and events. It is important that the team orchestrate a review to discuss existing or new ideas in different combinations. The team should encourage and promote the propagation of ideas from not only the team members but also from individuals who have specific knowledge of the issues.

Some creative tools that can be applied to the product safety and liability prevention initiative are:

- Brain Writing – building on each other's ideas

- Classic Brainstorming – creating sizable and better ideas

- Morphological Box – identifying all parts of the problem

- TILMAG – building ideal solutions through associations and analogies

- Pareto Analysis – analyzing failures to determine the vital few over the trivial many

- Force Field Analysis – identifying positive and negative effects of the forces that may cause failure

Once the organization has constructed the product safety review, selected team members can identify appropriate creative tools. These tools are used specifically to identify potential product failures that might exist in the user environment.

One of the major reasons for product failure is flawed design. It is caused specification errors such as inadequate knowledge of loads and stresses to which the product may be exposed, poor selection of materials used in fabrication, and lack of proper research of the intended application and user environment.

Another major reason for product malfunction is poor manufacturing practices. If the manufacturing processes have been inadequately developed, manufacturing equipment may cause burrs, sharp edges, poor welds, and insufficient heat-treating and plating. Any one of these manufacturing defects may cause the product to fail in the user environment and result in injury to the user.

As was discussed earlier, the maintenance factor can also result in operational failure. Many products require operational maintenance. If this maintenance is conducted improperly, at inadequate intervals, or simply not at all, then the product is subject to failure and the user to potential harm. Many users, particularly of products that serve a commercial market, elect to do the maintenance themselves. Cost issues, lack of time, and lack of know-how contribute to poor maintenance practice.

Sometimes product failure may be caused by exposure to variation in the environment. For example, a semi-truck may be exposed to excessive cold in the Alaska territory, which seizes the engine, freezes lubricants, and results in an engine that won't start. An excessively low temperature combined with weak antifreeze can crack an automobile's radiator and cause the metal piping to burst. Rain and snow can cause premature corrosion. Corrosion, excessive heat, strong winds, and other environmental conditions can result in product failure and, consequently, harm and peril to the user. Design and manufacturing disciplines must, therefore, embody a sound and effective product safety review comprising qualified team members.

Engineering standards are specified by the customer, by the manufacturer, by associations (NEMA, ASTM, ISO), or by governmental agencies. Design parameters such as temperature limits, load limits, stress limits, and other application criteria must be followed. If the person operating the product fails to follow these limits, the product may fail. For example, kitchen blenders, mixers, lawn tractors, and home gas generators have restrictions and limitations on duration of use. These types of products are designed to be used under limited conditions. If these limits are exceeded, the product may not withstand continuous excessive loads and may fail to operate. The failure could result in harm or peril to the user.

In earlier days, the solution to product liability was prevention; overdesigning a product was common. For example, the structural engineer would design a bridge with a four-factor load stress. If the anticipated total weight of all vehicles (including a calculated average of trucks, buses and cars) was 250,000 pounds, the maximum design parameter would be 1,000,000 pounds, or four times the total average weight.

The same criteria was used for maximum weight of an elevator, the seat weight of a wheelchair, the amperage of an electric generator, the wing stresses of an aircraft, and so on. The criteria for which the over-design was determined was called the *safety factor*. Engineers recognized that product is susceptible to manufacturing nonconformity, degradation over time, and misapplication and misuse. In order to protect the customer and safeguard against a product lawsuit, the engineer would design the product or system to support two or more times the actual foreseeable application.

This safety factor philosophy became the standard for product tolerance determination, and this philosophy is still the benchmark for today's product specifications. There is a caveat to using this as the only yardstick for all safety factors. Although the concept of safety factor is applicable in many product designs, other products may require multiple components in series or parallel in structure to assure a safe product. For example, an aircraft radar system should be designed to provide a subsystem as a backup. An automobile trunk is designed to be opened electronically by a device located at the driver's seat and mechanically by a latch on the trunk lid. For safety reasons, many cars today also provide a pull hatch that can open the trunk from inside.

There is hardly any product that does not require safety features incorporated into the design parameters. All pressure vessel devices, all electrical devices, all hydraulic devices, and many mechanical devices… the list goes on.

MALFUNCTIONS CAUSING FAILURES

Malfunction is the result of a condition that allows nonconformity of one or more characteristics and causes the product to fail. These malfunctions can be classified into six types of failure:

1. Mechanical
2. Structural
3. Pneumatic

4. Electrical
5. Power source
6. Hydraulic

Even though malfunctions are the cause of most product failure, it is the damage caused by the mishap that is the focal point of the lawsuit or insurance recovery and the focus of the case. For example, a bicycle cable breaks on a bike. This causes the brake to malfunction, and consequently causes the bike rider to lose control and sustain injury. This relationship between the malfunction (cause) and the injured person (effect) may not be quite as apparent as a direct relationship such as an electric knife blade separating from its holder (cause), resulting in a cut finger (effect).

However, oftentimes the cause-and-effect relationship is not clear. For example, a defective bearing of a floor sweeper *caused* oil to leak onto a factory production floor. An employee slipped on the oil and broke his arm. The employee was shuttled to the local hospital and the arm was repaired. The *effect* was a broken arm, but what was the true cause? Was it the oil on the floor, or was it the leak of the floor sweeper? Or was it something else, such as poor maintenance practices or no maintenance at all?

One of the tasks of the product safety team is to analyze the cause-and-effect relationship of potential malfunctions and examine the root cause of field malfunction. The team should be trained in analysis tools such as Fault Tree Analysis (FTA), Mapping, Flow Relationships, Circuit Logic Analysis, Interface Analysis, Fault Hazard Analysis (FHA), Failure Modes and Effect Analysis (FMEA), Failure Modes and Criticality Analysis (FMECA), just to name a few.

Members of the product safety team need not be an expert in all of these analytical tools but they should be aware of the tool's application and should know when to use it. Malfunctions are a common cause of failure and usually cannot be detected by using suitable design criteria at the design stage. Rather they are detected through analytical means in the reliability and simulated modes of testing or by field failure analysis methods. Depending on the product type, the applicable malfunction testing equipment should be readily available for evaluation and appraisal by engineering and reliability laboratory personnel. This data should be an integral part of the product safety team's assessment process. This would include mechanical, structural, pneumatic, electrical, power source, hydraulic, and any other malfunction category.

There are many types of product failure. We have, up until now, concentrated primarily on malfunctions, but other failures are also critical to the product safety issue. These are equally important and addressing them should be part of a formal and documented checklist reviewed by the product safety review team to resolve issues of product safety.

For example, a manufacturer of wheelchairs may want to assure that only fire retardant materials are used on the arms, seat, and back covering of all wheelchairs. This characteristic should be tested every so often based on a qualified sampling scheme. This nonflammable material classification should not be limited to wheelchairs, but should carry over to some types of protective clothing, furniture, electrical insulation material, hydraulic fluids, solvents, and whatever products are subject to flammable potentials.

Some of the most common hazards that could result in injury are sharp corners, broken surfaces, sharp burrs, broken connector wires, and numerous other non-dimensional characteristics. Some of these characteristics may not cause harm in one circumstance, but in another could result in injury to the user. For example, a metal guardrail on a cruise ship would most likely not cause an injury if the passenger were walking downward from the guardrail edge, but if the passenger was walking upward of the railing he or she could receive a severe cut from the sharp edge of the rail.

Some hazardous conditions cannot be totally eliminated, and sometimes it's simply too costly to completely eliminate all hazards. But to do nothing could expose the manufacturer to a product liability lawsuit. For example, a lawnmower is designed to cut grass by allowing the sharp blades to rotate. Under certain circumstances, involving normal operation or misuse, this could injure the operator. However, design changes could be made to minimize this hazardous condition. One way to prevent an accident is to include a feature that shuts the mower off automatically if the operator's hands leave the handle. The same feature applied to a lawn tractor could stop the blades if the operator removes his or her body from the tractor seat.

Although many design parameters include fail-safe features that automatically shut off the circuit, engine, rotation blades, or whatever, other designs provide for a backup switch or lever that can deactivate the function. For example, a lever on the back of a lawn tractor disengages the transmission gear-wheel and prevents the tractor moving into drive mode.

The product safety review team should have, as one of its key activities, a checklist designed to assess what kind of hazard might cause harm to the end user of the product. The review agenda should provide sufficient time for the team to brainstorm all possible happenings and situations that might occur and develop ways to prevent them. There are many conditions in which a hazard would constitute a danger. For example, no guards on a machine, no rails around a large acid tank to prevent workers from falling in, no encasement around a reservoir to prevent liquid levels from overflowing, no filters or screens around an area to prevent foreign objects from entering that area, no thermal insulation around hot sources such as welding machines, industrial baking ovens, or heat treating furnaces.

It is essential that the product safety review team take the time to evaluate all events that might generate a hazard condition and at what level that hazard would constitute a danger. This activity should be conducted not only from the product standpoint, but also from the standpoint of the working environment in the manufacturing facility. These are two distinct hazard analysis functions, but both can prevent harm or peril and both could protect the organization from a lawsuit.

HOW TO PERFORM A PRODUCT SAFETY EVALUATION

This evaluation is a key responsibility of the product safety review team, and members should be selected for ability, experience, knowledge, and creativity to visualize potential hazards. Each member should be trained in statistical application, problem solving, and evaluation techniques and each member should be empowered to perform the product safety evaluation.

We recognize that no product is completely safe and that a product designed and made correctly could be intrinsically hazardous. The team must be aware of all these possibilities.

Each product is unique with its own set of features and the team must determine the possibility of hazard for each feature. After each hazard is identified, the team must solicit a resolve and test for effectiveness.

Willie Hammer developed a checklist of potential hazards originally published in *Product Safety Management and Engineering* (Prentice Hall). The list includes the following:

- Toxic Materials
- Vibration and Noise
- Pressure Vessels
- Mechanical Hazards
- Heat and Temperatures

- Flammability and Fires
- Explosives and Explosions
- Chemical Reactions
- Electrical Systems
- Acceleration

The following questions address some evaluation examples of potential hazards.

Toxic Materials

1. Does the product contain material that could be harmful if inhaled or swallowed or absorbed into the skin?

2. Can the material increase toxic effect if it is mixed with another substance?

3. Can deterioration result in a product that could be toxic?

4. Can combustion of the material result in a product that could be toxic?

5. If the material is hazardous in an enclosed space, does the warning indicate conditions in which it is safe to use?

Vibration and Noise

1. Is it practical to reduce the noise in the product?
2. Is it possible to use sound-absorbing material to reduce noise emissions?
3. Are moving parts mounted and secured to avoid or minimize vibration?
4. If vibration sources cannot be eliminated, is the product provided with isolators or dampers?
5. Have fastened parts been tightened securely to prevent motion between parts?

Pressure Vessels

1. Is the pressure vessel designed and manufactured to applicable code?
2. Has the pressure vessel been proof-pressure and/or burst-pressure tested?
3. Is there a means of preventing a reversed installation or connection?
4. Is flexible hose protected against chafing, twisting, or other damage?
5. Does the container or any line that might be over-pressurized have a relief valve, vent, or burst diaphragm?

Mechanical Hazards

1. Have sharp points, sharp edges, and ragged surfaces not required for the function of the product been eliminated?
2. Does the product have pinch-points, rotating components, or other moving parts that must be guarded?
3. Are ventilation openings small enough to keep fingers away from dangerous places?
4. Have locknuts, lock-washers, safety wires, cotter pins, or similar devices been used to secure fasteners of critical assemblies so that they will not loosen or separate?

Heat and Temperature

1. Is there a source of heat in the product that has a temperature high enough to cause burns?

2. Is there any material that will become brittle and break easily when subjected to a low temperature?

3. Will changes in temperature cause undesirable loosening or binding of parts?

4. Is a relief valve necessary on a pressure system to prevent venting of fluid if the temperature increases its pressure?

5. Are pressurized containers shielded from direct rays of the sun?

Flammability and Fires

1. Does the product contain or use combustible material?

2. At what temperature will combustible material ignite?

3. Is it practical to substitute a nonflammable material for one that will burn?

4. If the combustible material is a liquid, what is its flash point?

5. Does the product contain a monitoring device to indicate the presence of fire or conditions that might precede a fire?

Explosives and Explosions

1. Does the product contain explosive or any material that can act as an explosive?

2. Is the explosive protected against inadvertent activation?

3. Are the explosive and initiating devices suitably marked with warnings?

4. If the main charge needs an initiating device to be activated, is the initiating device separated from the main charge?

5. Does the gas contain an odorant that will permit detection of leakage?

Chemical Reactions

1. Is there any material present that will react with the moisture in the air or with any other source of water or moisture?

2. Will the product injure skin it comes into contact with?

3. If the material is used in the home and might injure a child, is the container provided with a child-resistant opening?

4. Does the product contain a material that is hypergolic (reacts to initiate a fire) with any other material?

5. Will the product cause injury to eyes by chemical reaction?

Electrical Systems

1. Are voltage and amperage levels high enough to cause shock injury?

2. Is there any point at which a person could touch a live wire or conductor when the product is activated?

3. Is any surface, other than a heating element, hot enough to burn a person or ignite a material?

4. Are there any places where lint, grease, or other flammable material can accumulate?

5. Can the product be inadvertently activated to cause injury?

Acceleration

1. Will the product or any of its parts be in motion and thus subject to acceleration or deceleration effects?

2. Can structural members of the product be overloaded by sudden impact, stoppage, or dynamic load?

3. Is the lifting or lowering device designed to start and stop smoothly to prevent dynamic overloading?

4. Is there a condition in which a high-speed device is rotating strong enough that might cause fragments if the device fails in motion?

5. Can the speed of a rotating device be kept within safe limits?

Miscellaneous Hazards

1. Will contamination affect safe operation of the product?

2. If contamination might affect the performance of the product, are the critical parts hermetically sealed or otherwise protected?

3. Could the product emit contamination that could injure vegetation or marine life that might come into contact?

4. Have instructions been provided for keeping the product clean and frequency of cleaning?

5. Is there material in the product that acts as a fungus or bacterial?

Other questions directly salient to a specific product can be incorporated into the product safety evaluations process. It is the responsibility of the product safety team to examine all possible hazards that might cause harm or peril to the end user or cause the product to prematurely fail.

In order to maximize a product safety evaluation it is important to practice the following rules:

1. Don't rush the hazard analysis process (specifically the evaluation process).

2. Consider potential hazards that could arise.

3. Write them down and discuss each with the team.

4. Study possible effects and possible causes.

5. Determine the solutions to each hazard.

6. Implement action to eliminate the hazard.

7. Validate the implementation for effectiveness.

DESIGN FOR A FAIL-SAFE PRODUCT

The primary objective of a fail-safe design is to eliminate, or at least minimize, the possibility a product will leave the facility with a failure that will cause harm to the user. In most applications the main objective of a fail-safe design is to protect the user. It also protects equipment and the environment in which the product is used.

The most common fail-safe example is a home circuit breaker. The circuit breaker or fuse opens when the electric load is exceeded; a "short circuit" occurs. This function will inactivate the system and prevent an overload, which could result in a house fire. This example can also be applied to the electrical system of an automobile or any other electrical system.

Inactivation simply means that the product will stop functioning and become inoperative before it causes harm to a person or danger to an environment, but inactivation is only one of many fail-safe concepts.

Some products have the opposite fail-safe arrangement. Some have a built-in protection that permits the product to continue to function (for example, certain limit switches, two-hand controls, key interlocks, signal coding, photoelectric devices, and so on). Many stamping, cold heading, and injection molding manufacturers have presses that are designed to operate only when an operator uses both hands to push on dual buttons. This method assures that both hands are free from the press operation.

Some products are designed to signal the user if the product becomes near a non-function state or a hazard condition is forth coming. For example, just before the battery wears out on a fire alarm a signal sounds, announcing that the fire alarm will fail to operate. At a railroad crossing, a flashing light and a closing gate announce the arrival of an oncoming train.

Many products are designed to incorporate a redundant feature. For example, a twin-engine aircraft is designed so that if one engine fails the pilot can still manage to land safely. This feature becomes even more significant for a large jet liner. The same redundancy theory can be applied to a large ship with several engines or to a hospital operating room that relies on a back-up generator that automatically activates if the electric power goes.

Some products are designed with back-up safety features. In the lumber industry the cutting down of trees is a dangerous job that requires the use of special heavy equipment called a "yarder." A yarder is designed to pull a large tree from difficult conditions on hilly or mountainous terrain. If the hydraulic brakes failed, it would expose the operator and the ax-men to a dangerous situation; a back-up foot brake can operate the yarder manually.

Although most fail-safe designs are well thought out, other forces can cause harm to the user of the product; if they are not properly addressed, injury may result. Rain, snow, and ice are such factors. Under normal conditions an aircraft will function without a problem, but an excessively cold day with snow may cause icing on the wings of a plane. This ice can result in an unsafe condition, so aircraft mechanics will de-ice the wings before take-off. Likewise an automobile tire might have been designed with a fail-safe rubber that, if punctured, will seal itself; rain or snow may cause the tire to slide on the pavement, causing injury to the passengers. Special winter tires or rain tires are an option.

Thousands of products are produced that could result in injury to manufacturing personnel (operators, processors, assemblers, and so on), or to users of the products; these products should undergo an in-house product safety review initiative. Thousands of other products probably will not cause harm and injury to the user and perhaps not even to manufacturing personnel (for example, a drink coaster, a paperback book, a door wedge, an artificial flower, a birthday card). But even though these items may not cause harm, they should be reviewed for such an occurrence and documented…regardless of how minor it may seem.

There are many different types of product failure, and we have touched on just a few. The important message to take from this chapter is that failure can exist when we least expect it. The only way to be assured that these potential failures will not cause harm to the user of the product, or the operator of the product, is to analyze the cause of a failure and the effect it might have in the application and environment in which it is used. Some may be evaluated and declared to be non-hazardous; these need not be examined further. But products that have been assessed to be harmful, if failure occurs, must be designed and manufactured to provide for safe application.

Regardless of whether the assessment has determined the product to be in a safe state, with no further safety action needed, or whether the product has been determined to be subject to failure that might cause injury or peril to the user, the assessment process must be documented and all data and information must be recorded and retained. A designed program comprising product failure analysis and data documentation, supported by an effective quality assurance and reliability system, is critical to building a foundation for producing a safe product.

13

Warnings and Cautions

Warnings and cautions have a common objective. Both are communication processes meant to protect the customer from harm and/or loss of application intent. But each has a distinct function that must be addressed. This chapter is structured to first focus on "Warnings" as a stand-alone subject and then drill in on "Cautions."

Manufacturers have a proclivity to focus on meeting design requirements and developing an internal production system to comply with design parameters. A product may comply with design and process requirements and still be considered nonconforming in the eyes of the law if the warnings or warranties are inadequate. It is difficult to judge whether your warning is sufficient to eliminate or minimize the possibility of harm to the product's user. And it is difficult to determine whether the warranty is sufficient to satisfy customer expectation as to the life of the product. We will focus on the warranty aspect in Chapter 14.

WARNINGS

Unlike the cost in time and money that a manufacturer must commit in order to meet the four stages of the product's life cycle, warnings are relatively inexpensive to produce and implement. Manufacturers sometimes use them to protect the user and bypass the expense of redesigning the product or adding features to the manufacturing processes. However, some manufacturer fear that such warnings might expose the company to negative publicity and they are reluctant to incorporate warning verbiage onto the product or instruction manuals.

Not displaying a warning message on the product creates the risk that its absence may result in potential harm if the user misuses or abuses the product or if a foreseeable or even an unforeseeable danger results. A warning is an effective method of protecting the user from a possible mishap that might result from improper use, but manufacturers should not perceive warning as a substitute for a product safety review or as an inexpensive alternative design.

The courts have been quite generous in their view of warnings as a way to protect the user from harm and as an effective method of minimizing manufacturer liability. But organizations should use warnings only when all reasonable design parameters have been evaluated as to the criticality of the characteristic in question. Although a warning can be an effective safeguard against user injury, it does not necessarily protect the manufacturer from liability. A plaintiff's attorney may, through expert witnesses, prove that a simple design change would, in fact, prevent such an injury.

A warning can be used to draw attention to a potential hazard or product malfunction, and it can be coupled with an instruction to prevent injury or malfunction from occurring. However, it is important to recognize the difference between a warning and an instruction. Webster's New World Dictionary defines a *warning* as "something that serves to warn." It is designed to caution about certain acts that may result in danger. An *instruction* is defined as "something taught as an order or directions."

Many products have warnings on both the product and the service and/or maintenance procedures manual. Other products may elect to place a warning in the instruction manual. Regardless of which document is used to incorporate the warning, it should be clearly defined and easy to read. If the product is used globally, the warning should be in the appropriate languages. Many product manuals are written in several languages, as are labels affixed to the product and product packaging. Sometimes a single document serves several models.

For example, a gas-fired condensing furnace may have two or more model types on the front page with a photo or drawing of each. This visual aid helps the customer determining which model applies to them. The front page may start with a note that states "This furnace is a highly specialized piece of equipment; read the following instructions carefully and completely." Directly below the note there may be a "safety consideration" subtitle, a subset of the warning part of the document.

The safety considerations might include words such as this: "Installation and servicing of heating equipment can be hazardous due to gas and electrical components. Only trained and qualified personnel should install, repair, or service heating equipment." It can also suggest that untrained personnel can perform basic maintenance functions such as cleaning and replacing air filters, but that all other operations must be performed by trained service personnel. Another caution would be to make sure that a fire extinguisher is available during startup and adjustments.

These safety considerations are similar to warnings and are often considered a warning. In the aforementioned example the warning would read something like the following:

WARNING: The ability to properly perform maintenance on this equipment requires certain expertise, mechanical skills, tools, and equipment if you do other than those procedures recommended in the User Manual. A FAILURE TO FOLLOW THIS WARNING COULD RESULT IN DAMAGE TO THIS EQUIPMENT, SERIOUS PERSONAL INJURY, OR DEATH.

In the same manual it is common to have multi-warnings. One warning might be very generic, while another might be more specific to the user. For example:

WARNING: Never store anything on, near, or in contact with the furnace, such as:

1. Spray or aerosol cans, rags, brooms, dust mops, vacuum cleaners, or other cleaning tools

2. Soap powders, bleaches, waxes or other cleaning compounds; plastic or plastic containers; gasoline, kerosene, cigarette lighter fluid, dry cleaning fluids, or other volatile fluids

3. Paint thinners and other painting compounds, paper bags or other paper products

A failure to follow this warning can cause corrosion of the heat exchanger, fire, personal injury, or death.

CAUTIONS

In addition to the warning notations are caution notations. For the gas furnace example, a caution might read:

CAUTION: Be sure the motor is properly positioned in the blower housing. The motor oil ports must be at a minimum of 45 degrees above the horizontal centerline of the motor after the blower assembly has been reinstalled in the furnace.

Complex products such as gas furnaces, lawn tractors, and snow blowers have many component parts and require multi-component instructions. These documents are often several pages long and very detailed in covering warnings and instructions; others are short and cover the warnings that are integrated into the instructions.

For example, a remote transmitter used to open and close a garage door is another complex product, but due to simplistic design parameters, the warnings and the instructions can appear on a single page with room to repeat the material in three languages. Likewise, the wireless keypad warning and instruction will fit on a single page. The following are examples of remote transmitter and wireless keypad warnings:

REMOTE TRANSMITTER

WARNING:

Moving door can cause serious injury or death.

- **Do not** install transmitter unless the door operator's **safety reverse** works as required by the door operator's manual.

- Wall control must be mounted in sight of door at least 5 feet above floor and clear of moving door parts.

- **Keep people clear** of opening while door is moving.

- **Do not** allow children to play with the transmitter or door operator.

If safety "reverse" does not work properly:

- **Close door then disconnect operator** using the manual release handle.

- Do not use transmitter or door operator.

- Refer to *Door and Door Operator Owner's Manual* before attempting any repairs.

Electrical shock can cause serious injury or death.

- Power cord must be unplugged before attaching any wires.

- Be sure wire ends do not touch each other or other terminals.

If you have questions or if you need a manual, contact the distributor or manufacturer of the operator.

WIRELESS KEYPAD

WARNING:

A moving door can cause serious injury or death.

1. Keep people clear of opening while door is moving.

2. **Do not** allow children to play with wireless keypad.

3. During programming, the door opener could begin to run; stay away from the moving door and its parts. To keep the door from moving, close the door and disconnect it from the opener by pulling the emergency release cord.

If safety "reverse" does not work properly:

1. **Close door and disconnect the opener** using emergency release cord.

2. **Do not** use door opener, remote controls, or wireless keypad.

3. Refer to *Door and Door Opener Owner's Manual* before attempting any repairs.

NOTE: These warnings were taken directly from Genie operating instructions.

In both the remote transmitter and the wireless keypad documents the warnings were, in part, written as instructional warnings. The warning was designed to discuss how the user can be safe from harm.

The gas furnace and the garage door opener equipment were two examples of the thousands of products requiring warnings either attached as a label to the product, in a manual document, or both. All products produced by a manufacturer, an assembler, or a distributor should be reviewed by the engineering group, reliability group, or product safety committee to determine whether a warning is needed and that specific contents and safety concerns are covered in detail.

There is not a set rule for how to warn users of product safety issues, but failure to warn in any reasonable form is considered a non-conforming flaw by the court system. Failure to warn can be as much a liability concern as a design or manufacturing defect. Many organizations will use WARNING, CAUTION, and DANGER to draw user attention to the concern. Regardless of the wording or the method used to describe safety concerns, the cause of the concern and the method of safeguarding against it are the primary drivers behind the warning notation.

Although the warning label and/or operating manual might use CAUTION and DANGER or a simpler warning to alert the user, it should follow a basic format to describe the concern:

• The concern of the safety issue

• The possible outcome

• The recommended action to avoid the outcome

Note: The warning must be located in a place that the user can readily see, and it must be clear in its wording. The fewer the words used in the warning message the better. But the fewer words used must not deter from the warning's intent.

Warning symbols can be an effective way to illustrate the warning concern, but they should be used in an understandable manner that does not cause confusion. One way to test the effects of a warning symbol is to select ten people at random who have no direct relationship with the product and quiz their understanding. If for any reason one or more do not clearly understand the message, question their confusion and revisit the warning communiqué. After you have made the necessary improvements, retest the warning.

If the warning is on a product label it is recommended to test the label at different temperatures and under excessive environmental conditions to verify that the label will remain affixed to the product. A warning has one basic purpose: to warn the user of harm that may arise if the product is used erroneously. A warning it is not intended to replace or substitute for a poor design or for the organization's attempt to save money by lessening the quality and reliability of the product.

Warnings serve to protect the user against foreseeable harm and misuse or abuse of the product by the customer. Warnings are not a protector against unforeseeable harm or lack of good manufacturing practices or poor product design.

14

Warranties

Warranties are simple guarantees. They are an agreement that secures the existence or maintenance of something. The product warranty is an organization's pledge that they will repair or replace a product within a specific period of time. The company will stand behind the quality and reliability of their product for any flaws that might become apparent within that time period.

There are basically two types of warranties:

1. Express Warranty – A statement by a manufacturer, distributor, or dealer (in writing or verbally) that guarantees the presence of safety features and that the product will function as intended for a specific period of time.

2. Implied Warranty – The implication by a manufacturer, distributor, or dealer that a product is suitable for a specific purpose or use, is in good condition, and is implied to be safe.

The breach of an express warranty would claim the defendant is liable for injury caused by a breach of a verbal or written agreement that the product will perform as intended and not result in injury to the plaintiff. The plaintiff must prove that there was a breach of the agreement, and that the breach resulted in the plaintiff or an ancillary party being injured.

The defendant would have to prove that there was no contractual relationship between the plaintiff and defendant, that any contractual relationship had expired, or that the plaintiff was negligent in using the product. There are other common defenses such as disclaimers or limitations of warranties, but the primary defense is that the customer misused the product and there was no breach of the warranty.

The breach of an implied warranty would claim the defendant is liable for a product found to be unsafe or not fit for the ordinary purpose for which it was marketed, and that it was the cause of injury or condition that led to injury.

In counterpoint, the defendant must prove that the product was reasonably safe when it left the defendant's possession and that the plaintiff's negligence caused the injury or condition that led to the injury.

A manufacturer's express warranty generally limits the time the warranty is in effect, the equipment or portions covered, and the extent of replacement: labor, parts, or both. An implied warranty has no such limitations.

Warranties for consumer products are usually printed on quality paper, often with an artwork border and similar wording. This type of warranty is usually classified as either a "full warranty" or "limited warranty." Full warranty means that the manufacturer will repair or replace any defective product without charge to the consumer; the warranty is not limited in time. If the manufacturer has been unable to make an adequate repair, the consumer may choose between a refund and a replacement. The full warranty also provides that not only the original purchaser, but any subsequent owner of the product during the warranty time period, is entitled to make a claim.

A limited warranty is a warranty that has specific conditions that limit the warranty claim. For example, a limited warranty may exclude labor costs or it may include deductions for wear (such as a tire or car battery). The limited warranty may also require the purchaser to pay for transportation expenses, and it may be limited to the original buyer only and not subsequent owners.

The limited warranty is the most common warranty of the express warranty category. Most manufacturers will incorporate the limited warranty in the owner's manual or the operator's manual. The warranty is usually enclosed within a square or rectangular border, but it can be identified as simply a heading stating "warranty" in bold letters. The following three limited warranties are examples of terminology that might be used. *Note: Each one of the examples has an exclusion paragraph.*

The first example is the Delta limited warranty (Delta is one of the top brands in the faucet market). The limited warranty covers fifteen models and two series of their faucet products.

Lifetime Faucet and Limited Warranty	
All parts and finishes of the Delta® Faucet are warranted to the original consumer purchaser to be free from defects in material & workmanship for as long as the original consumer purchaser owns their home. Delta Faucet Company recommends using a professional plumber for all installation & repair. Delta will replace, FREE OF CHARGE, during the warranty period, any part or finish that proves defective in material and/or workmanship under normal installation, use & service. Replacement parts may be obtained by calling x-xxx-xxx-xxx. This warranty is extensive in that it covers replacement of all defective parts and even finish, but these are the only two things that are covered. LABOR CHARGES AND/OR DAMAGE INCURRED IN INSTALLATION.	REPAIR, OR REPLACEMENT AS WELL AS ANY OTHER KIND OF LOSS OR DAMAGES ARE EXCLUDED. Proof of purchase (original sales receipt) from the original consumer purchaser must be made available to Delta for all warranty claims. THIS IS THE EXCLUSIVE WARRANTY BY DELTA FAUCET COMPANY, WHICH DOES NOT MAKE ANY OTHER WARRANTY OF ANY KIND, INCLUDING THE IMPLIED WARRANTY OF MERCHANTABILITY. This warranty excludes all industrial, commercial & business usage, whose purchasers are hereby extended. A five year limited warranty from the date of purchase. With all other terms of this warranty applying except the duration of the warranty. This warranty is applicable to Delta® Faucets manufactured after (then date given). **NOTE: The warranty continues with paragraphs that contain additional information.**

There are several caveats to the express warranty claims. For example, any promises made by the seller to the purchaser that relate to the product and become part of the agreement create an express warranty that the product shall conform to the promise. Any sample or model incorporated into the bargain creates an express warranty that all the products sold shall be the same as the sample or model. Also any description of the product made a part of the sale creates an express warranty that all the goods shall be the same as the description.

Manufacturers are cautioned not to oversell the product with unreasonable warranty claims. They should be careful not to make exaggerated claims for marketing purposes that might go beyond the limitations or capability of the product. An erroneous statement could result in litigation consequences. For example, if a manufacturer of a screwdriver knowingly sells a screwdriver that is intended for tightening screws and that screwdriver is used to open paint cans or for some other function, the manufacturer may be liable if a subsequent injury occurs as a result of the misuse.

One example of a product subject to multiuse is the pressure washer. Most pressure washer operating manuals have many warning notes, basically cautions about the danger of misusing the washer. The warranty of Sears, Roebuck and Company's Craftsman 2500 PSI MAX, 2.3 GPM MAX Pressure Washer is a limited warranty enclosed in the pressure washer's operating manual. It reads as follows:

CRAFTSMAN LIMITED WARRANTY

If this Craftsman product fails due to a defect in material or workmanship within two years from the date of purchase, return it to any Sears store, Sears Parts & Repair Service Center, or other Craftsman outlet in the United States for free repair (or replacement if repair proves impossible).

This warranty applies for only 90 days from the date of purchase if this product is ever used for commercial or rental purposes.

This warranty covers ONLY defects in material and workmanship. Sears will NOT pay for:

• Expendable items that can wear out from normal use within the warranty period, such as spray guns, hoses, nozzle extensions, nozzles, filters, and spark plugs

• Repairs necessary because of accident, or failure to operate or maintain the product according to all supplied instructions

• Preventive maintenance, or repairs necessary due to improper fuel mixture, contaminated or stale fuel

---

This warranty gives you specific legal rights, and you may also have other rights that vary from state to state.

Another example of a typical warranty is the Dirt Devil vacuum sweeper called the "Swivel Guide," manufactured by Royal Appliance Mfg. Company. This product is a versatile sweeper with a good quality reputation. The warranty is also a limited warranty and is enclosed in the owner's manual. It reads as follows:

LIMITED WARRANTY

To the consumer, Royal Appliance Mfg. Co. warrants this vacuum cleaner to be free of defects in material or workmanship commencing upon the date of the original purchase. Refer to your vacuum cleaner carton for the length of warranty and save your original sales receipt to validate start of warranty period.

If the vacuum cleaner should become defective within the warranty period, we will repair or replace any defective parts free of charge. The complete machine must be delivered prepaid to any ROYAL Authorized Sales & Warranty Service Station. Please include complete description of the problem, date of purchase, copy of original sales receipt and your name, address, and telephone number. If you are not near a warranty station, call the factory for assistance at USA x-xxx-xxx-xxxx / CANADA x-xxx-xxxx. Use only genuine Royal replacement parts.

The warranty does not mention unusual wear, damage resulting from accident, or unreasonable use of the vacuum cleaner. This warranty gives you specific legal rights and you may also have other rights. (Other rights may vary from state to state in the USA.)

Warning, cautions, and warranties are the way manufacturers, distributors, and dealers assure customers that they will receive a reliable and quality product that will not harm them if the product is used properly. It's also the way they warn customers about harm that would result from product misuse. Customer protection efforts were reinforced in 1975 with the passage of the Magnuson–Moss Warranty Act. This act basically superseded the Uniform Commercial Code and established rules requiring complete disclosure by the manufacturer and preventing deception in the marketing of a product.

These rules were established to incorporate into the warranty such items as the name and address of the warrantor, the products or parts covered, exceptions and exclusions from the terms of the warranty, elements of the warranty in words that are easy to understand and not misleading, and parts of the product that are not covered among other things. For further details refer to the Magnuson–Moss Warranty Act.

Many product liability lawsuits are not the result of design or manufacturing defect, but rather the manufacturer's failure to properly warn the user or provide a warranty. Manufacturers should make every attempt to design a safe product and assure, through good manufacturing practices and an effective quality management system, that the product will meet the application parameters and be safe and reliable for use. As a safeguard against possible harm, the manufacturer should also generate clear and precise warnings and a warranty that will communicate to the user exactly what items are covered and what items are not covered.

THE WARRANTY FALACY

Most manufacturers offer a warranty of some type, and they would have consumers think that the manufacturer is looking out for their best interests. They publish the warranty, often in bold print, and promote it as a 90-day or one-year guarantee of repair or replacement of a failed product at no extra cost to the customer…within this time period. Customers actually fall for this controversial and dubious pledge. Manufacturer would have consumer believe that they are giving more value as a goodwill gesture and standing behind their product.

However, the truth of the matter is they are actually saying, in a masked message, that the product is of poor quality and not reliable; that it is only guaranteed to function for a very short period of time. So what is the true life cycle of the product? Has the manufacturer conducted a root cause analysis, a mean time between failures (MTBF) study? Have they conducted a product failure mode and effects analysis (PFMEA) and a process FMEA? Have they conducted an environmental analysis or even a simulated environmental test? There are many more analytical tools and testing parameters that can be used to resolve problematical findings and improve the product's reliability.

These tools can assist in assuring the design and manufacturing processes are effective to guarantee that the product will function as intended without failure for a reasonable amount of time after the "infant mortality period," which is usually a month or two from the beginning of normal use. If these reliability tests are performed with sound and effective testing and an analytical plan, it is not unreasonable to expect a warranty of at least five years from the purchase of the product, particularly a large appliance or similar products.

Note: A $1000 appliance should last more than one year of warranty protection.

If the manufacturer had conducted reliability analysis and worked out all the problematic findings, they would have documented evidence that the product will meet or exceed the average failure period 99.865% of the time, with only a .135% failure before that time (an acceptable lower allowance rate of failure). But driven by lean manufacturing and Six Sigma initiatives (both excellent tools if properly applied), some manufacturers succumb to weaker, less expensive materials, cheaper and untrained labor, and unqualified processes. This action can lead to a warranty period significantly less than the consumer should expect. Should a dish washer fail fifteen months after purchase, or only three months after the warranty period? Should a refrigerator fail less than a year after the warranty period? Should a television fail nine months after the warranty period? These are actual events of products sold for more than a thousand dollars each, products that were marketed as a top quality and reliable. I believe purchasers would disagree with the manufacturer's marketing claim of a highly reliable product.

To prove this contention, Gookins Technologies, an organizational improvement firm, conducted a survey of 100 random consumers. They asked this question: "Have you ever had a product that failed right after the manufacturer's warranty period?" The results showed that 54% of those participating in the survey claimed they had purchased at least one product that failed within one year after the warranty period; 45% said they had a failure within their "extended warranty" period. These extended warranties cost up to several hundred dollars and make a significant profit for the manufacturer and the retailer and higher commission for the retail salespeople.

When the purchasers were asked if they would purchase another like product from the same manufacturer, they all said *no*. Purchasers believed that the manufacturer's product reliability and quality were unacceptable. The vast majority of the people in the survey classified the failed product as a large appliance (such as, refrigerator, stove, dishwasher, microwave, washer and dryer). One person in the survey purchased a toaster oven for $150 and after only two months out of warranty the oven stopped functioning. That person purchased another toaster oven, the same model at the same price, and it failed at about the same point beyond the warranty period. Later it was discovered that the manufacturer had stopped producing the product. The consumer will never purchase that brand name again because it represents poor quality.

Another person in the survey, frustrated with a well known appliance manufacturer, had purchased a refrigerator that failed less than a year after the one-year warranty period. That buyer contacted the manufacturer's warranty department, and asked the warranty supervisor if that model had a history of that type of failure. He was told that "it was none of his business and that data did not fall within that the warranty supervisor's purview." Needless to say, the product failure and that rude supervisor tarnished that manufacturer's image. The shopper pledged to never buy another appliance from that company. But that manufacturer is not the only participant in this warranty fallacy. Many organizations display the same problem, and many manufacturers simply do not realize that a poor warranty policy is costing them future sales.

Aftermarket parts are a "cash cow" for the manufacturer, and this cost is passed on to the consumer. The cost for a service call can range from $65 to $90, before parts and labor. This sales strategy can scare the consumer into an extended warranty because the potential product failure typically costs as much as $200 or more. All because the manufacturer does not want to assure that the product will properly function for more than a year.

An extended warranty is marketed as insurance against product failure within a specific period of time when the product is used under specific conditions. It protects beyond the typical one-year or 90-day manufacturer's warranty. Essentially, what the warranty offer is saying is this: "Our product cannot be guaranteed more than this short period of time; it is simply not reliable and it could fail within the manufacturer's warranty or the extended warranty period."

Of course the manufacturer would contend that failure can happen but that it is rare. What do the data show? Certainly those people surveyed may disagree.

Today the average refrigerator has an average life cycle of four and a half years, based on comments from retail sales people. Some store salespeople claim that this is due to government intervention and the elimination of Freon from the refrigeration process, which shortens refrigeration life. True or not, it is still the manufacturer's responsibility to design and manufacture a dependable and reliable product. Some older people claim that their heavy appliances lasted 20 years or more... back 30 years ago. One individual in the survey said he purchased a Kenmore refrigerator 34 years ago that is still running fine today. Another individual, not part of the survey, said her dishwasher, purchased 28 years ago, is still running and the dryer she purchased at the same time has needed only one new belt in all that time.

These stories are not uncommon. Many manufacturers would claim that these were not average users, that this is subjective feedback at most. Does it reflect negatively that the product reliability has taken a back seat to cheaper processes, cheaper labor, and cheaper materials used by manufacturers today?

If organizations continue to retain this unacceptable warranty practice and encourage consumers to purchase an extended warranty to protect against product failure before a reasonable product life cycle, then surely some manufacturers will step up to the plate and recognize that this practice is not acceptable to consumers. Using a quality and reliability plan to aggressively analyze failure data and causations, manufacturers should be able to resolve these issues and expand their warranty period to five or even ten years. This bold move could result in significantly increased product market share and improved profits. A manufacturer with a well planned advertising effort could drive the one-year warranty policy out of existence and lead the way to a paradigm shift in warranty policies. Hyundai and Kia both came out with a ten-year or 100,000 mile warranty and both subscribe to the philosophy of driving defects to zero.

The cost to initiate such a plan is incremental to the overall benefits. The aforementioned survey clearly indicates the anger and frustration felt by typical consumers about the existing warranty policies and the methods manufacturers use to obtain extended warranty revenue under the fallacy of providing protection against a potentially flawed product.

15

Final Thoughts

Product safety is a critical part of a manufacturer's overall objective, but not the main driver. The main objective of a manufacturer or distributor is to make and sell a product at a profit. Manufacturers and distributors that don't make a profit will not stay in business very long. This is a basic premise of any business. The profit incentive has a major impact on how executive management makes organizational decisions. It also affects the organization's stakeholders, including employees, suppliers, stockholders, and the community at large.

A manufacturer that loses money will normally act immediately to cut costs. The areas most vulnerable are quality assurance, materials management, preventive maintenance, and other ancillary activities such as product safety reviews and reliability engineering.

Many companies are profitable, but they are driven to be more profitable. They adopt Six Sigma, lean manufacturing, TRIZ, and other cost improvement programs. These cost incentive activities have a direct effect on the product safety function. Taken to the extreme, they could affect product safety to the extent that users are harmed by unsafe products. This would be counterproductive to the manufacturer's image and profitability.

A company's failure to recognize the gravity of the potential harm caused by a defective product or an improper application warning could result in a lawsuit and judgment that would financially devastate the organization. Many manufacturers and distributors have been forced into bankruptcy due to the lack of proper product safety actions. In some cases, executive management of an organization has been found guilty of criminal intent.

Even when the "malfunction" or "failure to warn" does not cause immediate injury or death to the user of a product (even in cases of misuse or abuse), the findings may trigger a product recall. The product recall may be based on government regulatory requirements, environmental mandates, or simply the potential of a hazardous condition.

The product safety review should be a continuous activity, not subject to cost savings' incentives but rather an integral part of the organization's objectives. To accomplish this, the product safety review must have its own mission statement. This statement should incorporate the four stages of the product life cycle (concept, pre-production, production, and post-production), and should outline how the product safety review agenda can assure that product is analyzed for potential harm conditions and corrective action put in place.

Product liability insurance coverage is a protection that every manufacturer must have to protect against an unforeseeable event that harms an end user. When a product defect is proven to be caused by manufacturer negligence and when the defect causes injury or death, a company can be sued for thousands or even millions of dollars; without product liability insurance, the company is exposed to the possibility of bankruptcy and the closing of its doors.

But this insurance is not cheap. It can cost the company thousands of dollars a year in annual premiums, even with high deductibles. Most insurance carriers require the manufacturer to have in place a sound, well documented product safety initiative before they consider a manufacturer for coverage.

Many companies feel that product liability insurance is too costly and they elect to self-insure and take on the risk themselves. Without a solid platform of product safety and product reliability disciplines, this decision could expose them to cost so high as to cripple the company.

The manufacturer must first consider where product liability prevention activities will fall in the organization. In many companies these functions will be part of either the engineering department or the quality assurance department. Regardless of where the responsibility lies for product safety and reliability, the company must follow a few basic steps.

Once this organizational structure has been defined, the product safety team must create a product safety checklist of questions to be examined and respond to each question. This exercise will determine the needed directions that must be put in place in order to achieve an effective safety initiative.

After deciding which discipline will be accountable for product safety, the next step is to fund a reliability group to properly perform the task. This includes the creation of a basic reliability laboratory for simulated testing and environmental analysis of proposed product or existing product modifications. In some cases it may be necessary to conduct "real-life" testing and evaluation. The testing, analysis, and evaluations should be done as quickly as possible, but the process should not be rushed.

Many organizations will pressure the product safety team and reliability group to sign off on their functions before all evaluations have been done. They may be attempting to beat the competition to secure marketplace advantage or reacting to financial pressure to keep operating cost as low as possible.

The product safety team should participate in all four stages of the product life cycle:

1. *The concept stage* – The product safety team should review first stage of the cycle to assess whether the proposed product can be produced in compliance with engineering specification or the customer's preliminary design. This is the time to resolve application issues and safety concerns.

2. *The pre-production stage* – At this stage, the design has been issued to prototype. The same product safety team should intervene and evaluate the new or modified product for compliance to customer and application requirements. The reliability function should participate to determine environmental and application compliance.

3. *The production stage* – At this stage the assurance function is critical. The team should review inspection and production testing data to determine whether problems exist. This is also the time to review a process failure mode and effect analysis (PFMEA) for validation.

4. *The post-production stage* – At this stage the product safety team reviews the product as it performs in the field and evaluates warranty claims and customer returns. The team should have a system in place to occasionally pull product from the field in order to evaluate the life performance and mean-time-between-failures (MTBF).

All four stages must be recorded and any issues resolved and documented.

The company must assure that all organizational processes are in place and that they are effective. They can create their own quality management system or they can incorporate a national or international quality management system such as ISO 9001 and ISO 9004.

It takes time and money to integrate product safety and reliability into an organization's operating structure, and it requires a commitment from executive management to assure its effectiveness. Failing to recognize the importance of product safety and reliability, and believing that the organizations can side-step potential product liability, is not wise.

Manufacturers must assess their products for safety and reliability, decide whether the potential for harm exists, and then develop a product safety and reliability initiative. The manufacturer of greeting cards may decide that a product safety plan is not needed, but a manufacturer of ceiling fans may elect to have a full-fledged product safety initiative. Each manufacturer should assess their product for liability exposure or involve an outside product liability prevention consultant.

Manufacturers and many American citizens would like to see changes in our legal system to stop the propagation of frivolous lawsuits. Frivolous lawsuits drive up the cost of goods manufactured and the price of products made and/or sold in the United States. This cannot continue. Until Congress passes a law to limit the amount a plaintiff can receive and to penalize plaintiffs for unfounded litigation, we cannot maintain a competitive advantage in the world market.

Until there are changes in the legal system, manufacturers will not be playing on a level playing field and must be defensive in the way they manufacturer and sell their products. Until there are changes in product liability law, manufacturers should have an effective product safety council and reliability group in place to function as the company's "watch dog."

Don't allow your organization to be subject to a lawsuit and/or product recall because you choose to ignore the possibility that your product may cause harm or peril to the user.

Glossary

abuse—Using the product in a manner that could cause harm or impair the function of the product.

assignable cause—The cause of a nonconformity that has been identified as the reason for the defects such as a dimension being out of tolerance.

batch number—An identification of chemical or other non-metallic material processes in a vat or other container, such as foods, drugs, plastic parts, and so on).

book-binding—The limits established in time, identification, or other methods for capturing recalled products.

champerty—An illegal agreement with a litigating party to meet the expense of a suit for a share in the proceeds.

chance cause—The determined cause of a defect that is not assigned to specific operation flaw, such as an unexpected electrical impulse.

concept diagram—The diagramming of the stages and gates a new product is proposed to move through from inception to shipment.

conceptual design parameters—The characteristics (including dimensional and visual) that have been specified for the design of a quality and safe product.

conceptual stage—The inception of an idea that can be designed into a product.

contingency—The term used in the legal profession to indicate a sharing of reward between plaintiff and attorney.

corrective action—The examination of nonconformity to determine the root cause of the defect and the action needed to resolve the problem.

continual improvement—The examination of an operational system for the purpose of making the system more effective, efficient, and reliable.

damage control—A method of communication by words and action meant to nullify, or at least minimize, damage to the company's image.

deep pockets—An organization or person that represents significant monetary value to a plaintiff.

defendant—An individual or organization being sued.

Design FMEA (Failure Mode and Effect Analysis)—A risk priority assessment technique.

disposition—The determination of action needed to process defective product (such as scrap, rework, return to manufacturer, and so on).

e-coating—An electrolysis process that coats a metal or plastic part.

end use—The final application of a product.

expert witness—A knowledgeable individual who can testify in court for either the plaintiff or the defendant.

express warranty—A statement by the manufacturer, distributor, or dealer that guarantees the presence of safety features and intended functions.

fail-safe design—A system that has been designed to prevent harm to the user of the product.

failure to warn—The failure to explain potential harm to the user if the product is used in an unsafe manner.

FEA (Finite Element Analysis)—A manual or computer-aided design parameter for calculating fatigue and stress conditions of a product.

feasibility study—An early-stage analysis of the potential marketing of the product and all its ramifications and concerns in its final application.

field—Where the product is being used.

forseeable use—How the product may be used and the purpose of its application.

full warranty—A promise that the manufacturer will repair or replace any defective product without charge to the consumer; not limited in time.

fuzzy front end—The inception of the product's development.

heat number—An identification of a metal material used in the fabrication of a product or component, such as steel, gray iron, ductile, and aluminum.

heat treating—The process of changing the molecular structure of a metal part.

implied warranty—The implication that a product is suitable and safe for a specific purpose or use.

infant mortality period—A short period of time at the beginning of the usage cycle for a product that is susceptible to premature failure.

infrastructure cost—The cost of all elements involved in manufacturing a product, such as equipment, buildings, electrical busing, and so on.

inherent product hazard—A hazard that exists in a product (such as a knife, saw, and lawn mower) under normal and intended usage.

ISIT (Initial Sample Inspection and Test)—An initial appraisal of a product before it is released to production to assure that the product is in conformance.

ISO 9001—A process-based quality management system that is a general guide to aid the manufacturer or service organization for the collection of data for establishing an effective system.

ISO 31000—A guide to recognize the value of risk management and related methodologies.

life cycle—The period of time a product is functional from the concept idea to its inoperative stage.

Likert method—A psychometric scale commonly used in research employing questionnaires or fixed-choice responses.

limited warranty—A warranty that has specific conditions that limit the warranty claim.

material cost—The cost of all the sub-components and raw materials required in the production of a finished part.

metal finishing—An electrolysis process that distributes metal on the surface of a metal or plastic part.

mistake proofing—An examination process that determines the reliability of producing a characteristic that is 100% conforming.

misuse—Using the product in a different manner than designed, resulting in harm to the end user.

multi-functional product—A product that has more than one function to meet customer requirements.

nuisance suit—A lawsuit that is not of significant value and less expensive to the defendant if settled out of court.

objective evidence—The actual witnessing of a procedure or instruction for compliance.

paper napkin design—A metaphor for the initial concept development stage to determine the feasibility of creating a new product.

plaintiff—An individual or entity suing for consideration.

post-production stage—The final stage of the product life cycle that evaluates the performance of the product in the field.

PPAP (Production Part Approval Process)—A critical assessment tool to assure that the first production run will be in conformance with all designated characteristics.

pre-production stage—An initial process of qualification assessment designed to judge the service capability of the product and the possible extreme application of the product.

preventive action—The examination of a potential flaw or defect and the action taken to prevent it.

preventive maintenance—The review and determination of production equipment and any ancillary functions that could impair the product quality if not maintained on a time or frequency cycle, and the recording and retention of the maintenance documentation.

Process FMEA (Failure Mode and Effect Analysis)—A risk priority assessment of the process in the manufacturing of a product.

process mapping—An evaluation of all processes required in producing a product. It has the objective of making a product in the most efficient and effective manner.

product analysis—The analysis of each operation of a product, conducted at the time of initial product release to production.

product design review—A review of a new or modified product by a team of company experts representing the disciplines of the organization.

product effectiveness—Determination that a product will function properly over a given period of time under normal conditions.

product liability—An event whereby an injury or financial loss results in individuals or a business seeking compensation.

product liability prevention system—A system developed to minimize the possibility of a product resulting in harm or peril to an end user.

product recall—The removal of a product that has been deemed to cause harm or impair the function of the product to the user.

product recall coordinator—Someone in middle or upper management who is trained and assigned to monitor and control the product recall campaign.

product safety—The functioning of a product under normal use that has been designed and manufactured to operate in a safe manner.

product safety council—A formal committee made up of the line and staff support people who review potential conditions concerning product safety.

product safety review—A small group of people who have been trained to examine a new or existing product for application safety features.

production stage—The actual processes used in the fabrication and/or assembly of a product.

prototype—A pre-production part or product, usually fabricated in a model shop under engineering control, that looks like and functions like a production part.

redundancy—A system that has more than one path to fulfill a desired result.

reliable product—A product that has demonstrated by either simulated or environmental testing that it will meet its intended use for a specific period of time.

risk analysis scale—A tool that can be used to make decisions about the gravity of potential risk and action that must be taken to eliminate or reduce the possibility of accident.

risk assessment—The overall process of risk identification, risk analysis, and risk evaluation.

risk identification—A process of discovering, recognizing, and describing risk.

risk treatment—A process to modify risk.

simulated environment—A laboratory-constructed device designed to duplicate the conditions of the environment to which the product will be exposed.

simulated environment testing—A test performed in a reliability laboratory that simulates the action function of the product in its application.

single-purpose product—A product that depends on only one function to work and meet the customer's requirements.

TRIZ (The Theory of Inventive Problem Solving)—A problem solving theory that is based on the experiences of people who have solved real problems using innovation and inventive concepts.

uncertainty—The deficiency of information related to understanding or knowledge of an event, its consequence, or likelihood.

unforeseeable use—The use of a product other than for its designed purpose (such as using a screwdriver to open a paint can).

voice of the customer (VOC)—The communication of the customer's expectations and requirements to the supplier.

warning—An effective method of protecting the user from a possible mishap that might result from improper use of the product.

workflow—The movement of the product from all stages of the processes to shipment.

About the Author

D r. E.F. "Bud" Gookins is an internationally known quality consultant and lecturer. He is president of Gookins Technologies Ltd., a quality systems and management consulting firm. Since 1962, he has developed and implemented quality systems and conducted numerous training programs in quality and management concepts for a diverse group of industries and service organizations.

He has held numerous leadership positions, including that of president and chief executive officer, of manufacturing organizations. He has lead corporate quality initiatives for Fortune 100 companies, and has sat on the board of directors for several companies. Dr. Gookins has lectured extensively, trained more than 20,000 people, and published more than 50 professional papers on human behavior, organizational development, and quality management systems and technologies—both domestically and internationally.

Dr. Gookins is a registered professional engineer, a certified quality management systems lead auditor, and a member of the National Society for Professional Engineers (retired). He is a "fellow," a past national officer, and is presently vice chair for "The Product Safety and Liability Prevention Group" of the American Society for Quality (ASQ). He participated on development committees for ASQ's certified quality engineer (CQE) and the certified mechanical inspector (CMI) credentialing programs. Bud is the co-founder of the Ohio Award for Excellence Council and past vice-chair of its board of trustees.

He has taught both graduate and undergraduate courses as an adjunct professor for the business college and the engineering college of several universities for more than 38 years. In his doctoral studies Bud focused on the impacts of human factors on quality and productivity performance. He has conducted behavioral research in this field and is the author of *The TASK Paradigm*.

Dr. Gookins has received many awards and recognition for his work in the quality profession, including the international acclaimed Edwards Medal for outstanding contribution to the quality management movement worldwide, the Grant Medal for educational pioneering in quality, the Ishihawa Medal for work in the humanistic aspects of organizational performance, and the Harry Lessig Award for contributions to inspection and testing technologies. He is a contributing author to the *Juran Quality Control Handbook,* fifth edition, McGraw Hill; contributing author to *The Product Liability Handbook,* Quality Press; a member and officer of the International TAG's 69 & 176 for ISO standards; and a member and officer of the Accredited Standards Committee Z1 for the United States.

Index

Page numbers in *italics* refer to figures and tables.

Belong to the Quality Community!

Established in 1946, ASQ is a global community of quality experts in all fields and industries. ASQ is dedicated to the promotion and advancement of quality tools, principles, and practices in the workplace and in the community.

The Society also serves as an advocate for quality. Its members have informed and advised the U.S. Congress, government agencies, state legislatures, and other groups and individuals worldwide on quality-related topics.

Vision

By making quality a global priority, an organizational imperative, and a personal ethic, ASQ becomes the community of choice for everyone who seeks quality technology, concepts, or tools to improve themselves and their world.

ASQ is...

- More than 90,000 individuals and 700 companies in more than 100 countries

- The world's largest organization dedicated to promoting quality

- A community of professionals striving to bring quality to their work and their lives

- The administrator of the Malcolm Baldrige National Quality Award

- A supporter of quality in all sectors including manufacturing, service, healthcare, government, and education

- YOU

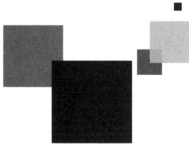
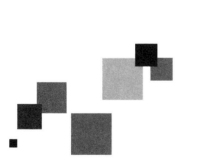

Visit www.asq.org for more information.

ASQ Membership

Research shows that people who join associations experience increased job satisfaction, earn more, and are generally happier.* ASQ membership can help you achieve this while providing the tools you need to be successful in your industry and to distinguish yourself from your competition. So why wouldn't you want to be a part of ASQ?

Networking

Have the opportunity to meet, communicate, and collaborate with your peers within the quality community through conferences and local ASQ section meetings, ASQ forums or divisions, ASQ Communities of Quality discussion boards, and more.

Professional Development

Access a wide variety of professional development tools such as books, training, and certifications at a discounted price. Also, ASQ certifications and the ASQ Career Center help enhance your quality knowledge and take your career to the next level.

Solutions

Find answers to all your quality problems, big and small, with ASQ's Knowledge Center, mentoring program, various e-newsletters, Quality Progress magazine, and industry-specific products.

Access to Information

Learn classic and current quality principles and theories in ASQ's Quality Information Center (QIC), ASQ Weekly e-newsletter, and product offerings.

Advocacy Programs

ASQ helps create a better community, government, and world through initiatives that include social responsibility, Washington advocacy, and Community Good Works.

Visit www.asq.org/membership for more information on ASQ membership.

*2008, The William E. Smith Institute for Association Research

ASQ Certification

ASQ certification is formal recognition by ASQ that an individual has demonstrated a proficiency within, and comprehension of, a specified body of knowledge at a point in time. Nearly 150,000 certifications have been issued. ASQ has members in more than 100 countries, in all industries, and in all cultures. ASQ certification is internationally accepted and recognized.

Benefits to the Individual

- New skills gained and proficiency upgraded
- Investment in your career
- Mark of technical excellence
- Assurance that you are current with emerging technologies
- Discriminator in the marketplace
- Certified professionals earn more than their uncertified counterparts
- Certification is endorsed by more than 125 companies

Benefits to the Organization

- Investment in the company's future
- Certified individuals can perfect and share new techniques in the workplace
- Certified staff are knowledgeable and able to assure product and service quality

Quality is a global concept. It spans borders, cultures, and languages. No matter what country your customers live in or what language they speak, they demand quality products and services. You and your organization also benefit from quality tools and practices. Acquire the knowledge to position yourself and your organization ahead of your competition.

Certifications Include

- Biomedical Auditor – CBA
- Calibration Technician – CCT
- HACCP Auditor – CHA
- Pharmaceutical GMP Professional – CPGP
- Quality Inspector – CQI
- Quality Auditor – CQA
- Quality Engineer – CQE
- Quality Improvement Associate – CQIA
- Quality Technician – CQT
- Quality Process Analyst – CQPA
- Reliability Engineer – CRE
- Six Sigma Black Belt – CSSBB
- Six Sigma Green Belt – CSSGB
- Software Quality Engineer – CSQE
- Manager of Quality/Organizational Excellence – CMQ/OE

Visit www.asq.org/certification to apply today!

Self-paced Online Programs

These online programs allow you to work at your own pace while obtaining the quality knowledge you need. Access them whenever it is convenient for you, accommodating your schedule.

Some Training Topics Include

- Auditing
- Basic Quality
- Engineering
- Education
- Healthcare
- Government
- Food Safety
- ISO
- Leadership
- Lean
- Quality Management
- Reliability
- Six Sigma
- Social Responsibility

ASQ Training

Classroom-based Training

ASQ offers training in a traditional classroom setting on a variety of topics. Our instructors are quality experts and lead courses that range from one day to four weeks, in several different cities. Classroom-based training is designed to improve quality and your organization's bottom line. Benefit from quality experts; from comprehensive, cutting-edge information; and from peers eager to share their experiences.

Web-based Training

Virtual Courses

ASQ's virtual courses provide the same expert instructors, course materials, interaction with other students, and ability to earn CEUs and RUs as our classroom-based training, without the hassle and expenses of travel. Learn in the comfort of your own home or workplace. All you need is a computer with Internet access and a telephone.

Visit www.asq.org/training for more information.